Love Conquers All

The Loving Light Books Series

Book 1: God Spoke through Me to Tell You to Speak to Him
Book 2 & 3: No One Will Listen to God & You are God
Book 4: The Sun and Beyond
Book 5: The Neverending Love of God
Book 6: The Survival of Love
Book 7: We All Go Together
Book 8: God's Imagination
Book 9: Forever God
Book 10: See the Light
Book 11: Your Life as God
Book 12: God Lives
Book 13: The Realization of Creation
Book 14: Illumination
Book 15: I Touched God
Book 16: I and God are One
Book 17: We All Walk Together
Book 18: Love Conquers All
Book 19: Come to the Light of Love
Book 20: The Grace is Ours

Also by Liane Rich

The Book of Love
For the Love of God: An Introduction to God
For the Love of Money: Creating Your Personal Reality
Your Individual Divinity: Existing in Parallel Realities
For the Love of Life on Earth
Your Return to the Light of Love: a guidebook to spiritual awakening

Loving Light

Book 18

Love Conquers All

Liane Rich

The information contained in this book is not intended as a substitute for professional medical advice. Neither the publisher nor the author is engaged in rendering professional advice to the reader. The remedies and suggestions in this book should not be taken, or construed, as standard medical diagnosis, prescription or treatment. For any medical issue or illness consult a qualified physician.

Loving Light Books
Original Copyright © 1996
Copyright © 2011 Liane

All rights reserved. This book may not be copied or reproduced in any form whatsoever, without written permission from the publisher, except for brief passages for review purposes.

ISBN 13: 978-1-878480-18-7
ISBN 10: 1-878480-18-9

Loving Light Books:
www.lovinglightbooks.com

Also Available at:
Amazon: www.amazon.com
Barnes & Noble: www.barnesandnoble.com

for Carol Ann

The information in this series is not necessarily meant to be taken literally. It is meant to *shift* your consciousness....

Foreword

Anyone immersed in the vast body of new metaphysical knowledge is aware of the virtual symphony of voices from channeled sources throughout the world – inspirational voices that may be artistic, poetic, philosophical, religious, or scientific. And now, out of these myriad New Age voices, comes a series of books by God, channeled through Liane, revealing the frank truth in all its glory and wonder, telling us how to cleanse our bodies, gain access to our subconscious minds, clear our other selves and march back to who we are – God.

In God's books you will be introduced to a loving, powerful, gripping, exciting, and often humorous voice that reaches out and speaks ever so personally to the individual reader. As the reader's interest deepens, invariably an intimate relationship to this voice develops. It is a relationship that lasts forever, and I am quite certain I do mean forever.

Here is an accelerated program, a no-holds-barred course, where God guides us and loves us, and as needs be recommends books to us and even a movie or musical piece along the way. He (She) enters our lives and sees through our eyes, seeming to enjoy the ride as He guides us back to US, back to ALL. Here is a voice that is playful and informative, that is humorous and serious, that is gentle and powerfully divine. It is a voice that knows no barriers or restrictions, a straightforward and honest voice that caresses us when we need the warmth and pushes us when we are immobilized.

In today's New Age literature there is an avalanche of information from magnificent beings of light, information that possesses us and compels us to look at our fears and express our love. In this series of books by God, you will find truly powerful methods for making this transition from toxicity to purity, from density to light, from fear to love, and from the delusion of death to the awakening to full life. You will experience in these books the love and the power of God for it is your love to express and your power to behold. Rarely will you see more lucid steps for transformation. Read these beautiful words and rejoice in our period of awakening, our return to Home.

John Farrell, PhD., LCSW. – Psychologist, Clinical Social Worker, Senior Clinician Psychiatric Emergency Services, U.C. Davis Medical Center, Sacramento. John is also a retired Professor – California State University, Sacramento, in Health Sciences and Psychology.

Love Conquers All

𝒜s you begin to read this book you will begin to shape a new part of you. You are creating you as we go along. Consciousness creates reality and you are becoming conscious and creating you (reality) as you do so. You are learning to see a new perspective and you are learning to believe in what you want as your truth. You are also beginning to see how you can be the one who loves you as well as the one who hates you.

As you learn to open up to more of your own wisdom and higher understanding, you will see greater parts of you taking on new roles and actually enjoying them. You are the most diverse and flexible being if you will give up and surrender to the flow. Most of you do not realize that you do not know how to flow. You think you do, but it is so new for you that you will not recognize it for some time. For now it is good enough that you concentrate on entering your body and allowing it to "be," without judging it to (greater) pieces.

You are already fragmented and split so much that it will take a great deal of work to replace all your fractured parts. You are growing out of fragmentation and into wholeness. This process takes time and love. You will take the time to heal, and you will love you all the more for doing so. You will be whole and non-fractured when you arrive at your own personal heaven.

You each have a state of bliss that is conducive to your own beingness. When you reach this state of bliss it will be quite joyful. It is not that your lives will have changed so much as it is the change in your perception of your life. I will give you an example of "perception shift." One day you are at work and one of your co-workers is sick. You offer to work extra hours and the boss says "No, I have it covered." You then begin to realize that the boss has never asked you to work overtime. You think to yourself "He doesn't like me or want me around." The next day you overhear the boss speaking to his assistant manager. He says specifically that he does not want the manager to call you in for extra hours. You feel even worse about yourself and your boss after hearing that. You now don't like him and are trying to defend yourself (in your head) as a good employee and worker.

Two days go by and your boss calls you into the office. He has a raise and a new position he would like to discuss with you. You freak out and think he is just trying to move you out of his area when, in actuality, he is in favor of giving you this new position because he feels you are a good worker and deserve a better position with less instead of more hours. In this position you will not have to deal with as much crap as you have in your old position. The boss didn't want to ask you to work overtime because he appreciates you and did not want to overwork you.

So; you feel under-worked and unappreciated, and so you will probably turn down the new position out of resentment and a belief that it is not as good as the old position. You feel that the boss does not like you and that he wants you out of the way. He would never offer you anything good, so you say "No" to a real gift, and you may never know how many of these gifts you have turned down in your life.

You are fragmented and you have parts of you who see everything as bad and do not recognize good. You may have a great relationship and think it is awful, because parts of you are busy acting out their dysfunction. I don't say this to confuse you more nor to frighten you. I say this to let you know how much healing will assist you in your day-to-day living. You are so defensive and afraid, that you are creating a hell for yourself. Your job here on earth is to create heaven. You will raise yourself up to a level of intensified light in order to see how good it will feel to be there forever. This will allow you to feel your own light. This will allow you to know that something good is in you trying to project out to your consciousness.

Once you have felt the light touch your life there is no turning back. You cannot return to the darkness when you feel the light on you for however brief the moment. You are full of this light. It is the love in you. It is not the love of a child, and it is not the love of your spouse or your dear pet. It is the love of you! When you can look upon you with the fondness and caring that you can show a beautiful newborn, or a loving pet, or a gentle spouse, you have arrived. When you can literally feel your love for yourself, you are turning away from hatred and low self-esteem.

Do you know how it is when a mother or father loves a child to the extent that they see their child as the most beautiful child in the world? You will love you with that same intensity. You will begin to see you as you truly are for the first time ever. You will see you through the eyes of love. Love creates beauty, love conquers all fear, and love opens up to the darkness and allows it to move freely to a new position. You will find your freedom in "love." You will find your bliss in "love" and you will find your heaven on earth in "love."

You are beginning now. It starts with opening up to your own self. It starts with going in you to see who and what you carry inside. Clean you out and you will set free your love. Love is trapped behind and under all your "should haves" and "could have" done this or been that. You are you for a reason. Allow you to be you!

❀

As you go through life, you begin to accumulate layers of beliefs and judgments. Most of these are composed of past beliefs regarding past situations and, therefore, your future becomes part of your past and you get stuck in a cycle. Once you begin to clean out and change old beliefs and layers of programming, you begin to create a very subtle but mild shift within the consciousness of your own soul. You begin to create a new possibility or a new passageway to the future or "your future." You create by changing and rearranging and being thoughtful or "thought filled."

Fill your head with thoughts and beliefs and you will create an event. Clear your head and you will see no new events. Events come from within you and are created by "shifts" which take place in you. It is like an instrument that is used to decorate a cake. You squeeze the tube and go in circles with your hand while holding the tube, and you make a design on your cake. Well, in creation, you go in circles and squeeze out what is in you. You call the circles cycles, and you create patterns by making your cycles. Change your cycles and you change your pattern or what you create.

As you learn to create from joy you will move into a new cycle. You can have sorrowful cycles, and you can empty yourself of the pain causing your sorrow and you will begin to have or create joyful cycles. This does not occur overnight. It is a built up process, and it is a taking-off of the buildup that creates the desire to be free of its weight. You take off one layer and it triggers the desire to remove the next. You see, these layers are restricting your soul and your soul has the desire to be "free." You may not know this on a conscious level, but, then again, you may! It depends on how often you communicate with your soul. Do you have the time to communicate with you or are you too busy? Oh well, it's your show! You get to direct, produce and play all the parts. You can stay stuck in cycles and patterns, or you can assist your soul in releasing and clearing enough debris to "lighten" some of your load.

How do you assist your soul? Well, it's very easy and not too exciting, so I doubt that you will get right to it. However for those of you who are ready, you may wish to review everything in this series regarding health and diet and lack of cigarette smoke and lack of drugs and lack of alcohol. Did you ever notice how you lack certain things in your life but those things are usually never prosperous? You seem to have lots of "lack" such as pain (or lack of physical well-being), or such as addictions (or lack of mental well-being). All of your lacks have to do with what is good for you, and your abundance seems to be reflected in ill health and addiction and pain and judgment.

We need to create lots of good health and well-being. The best way to promote something is to create lots of it. Do lots of healthy, loving, nurturing things for you and these things will begin to grow in your life. You will begin to see the percentages of drug users and addictive tendencies diminish as your soul begins to heal. You have a big hurt in your heart and your heart generates love and houses your soul energy. Love does not hurt you or anyone else. Pain is pain and it is generated by extreme pressure or resistance. It can be physical, mental, emotional, psychic or any number of other forms.

Pain is not you. You are learning to be pain-free by learning to care for and love you. You do not require drugs. Drugs and cigarettes and alcohol and chemicals do not heal you, they do not love you and they do not make your cells healthy and strong. Why do you think you put things in you that do not assist you in healing your soul? Think about it. Heal your soul and you heal your link to God. God is your power source. How can you not want to clean out you and take good care of you?

You die from not caring. You die from abuse and you die from neglect. Others tend to neglect you because you are registering and projecting neglect. Others tend to hate you because you are hating you. Did you know that you hate you? Would you hate someone (even secretly) if you knew that 'that someone' did not care enough to ensure your health and well-being? You are so afraid of offending others that you don't care how often you offend yourself. Your "self" is tired of being offended and disregarded and abused emotionally by you.

You bully you and push at you and this is what is about to change. Why do you think that so many parts begin to fail in the human body? You can only drag a dog on a leash for so long before that dog will rebel and stop! You stop. Your body stops running and quits on you. It drops dead. You still won't quit pushing it to go. You revive bodies and kick start them with instruments. Why can't you let the body go after you have given it nothing but grief for an entire lifetime?

You are consciously unhappy with your body size and often stature, so why fight so hard to hold on to it? Why not let it go? What is all the fuss about having a good-looking body if you only stuff it full of chemicals and force it to go even when it wants to not move? How can you break this cycle of physical, mental and emotional abuse by you to your body? It is easy... love you enough to take care of you. You say you don't have the time because you have to pay the bills and feed the kids. I say make time! If you were paid three billion dollars a year to maintain a prize 'being' like you with only the best of pampering and care, you would make the time even if you had other things to do.

For money you make time and for a new car you make time. You all have something that excites you enough that you would drop everything else and run. I want you to get excited about you. You have just moved into the most gorgeous new mansion and you are going to take excellent care of it. It is the home that was just given to you, and you will not receive a new home if this one burns down or is destroyed by floods. So I suggest, since you don't get a second home, that you take excellent care of this one.

Now; it's time to review: learn to stop judging you. Learn to love you. Learn to accept you. Learn to put positive thoughts in you. Learn to talk nicely to you. Learn to not poison you. Learn to appreciate you and, above all, learn to know you. To know you is to love you, for you are God and God is love. You tap into God; Love; Light; the Source of All That Is, right through you. Isn't that amazing? You had no idea how valuable you are, now did you?

※

As you learn to know the difference between love and loathing, you will begin to see how you have not been so good to you. You will begin to see how you have never been taught how to treat you with respect and admiration. Once you learn to recognize that you are dear and valuable, you will take whatever time is necessary to preserve and care for you. You will be gentle with you and you will see how you need you to live in.

Without you, you have no place to live. Without you, you have no place to stay. Without you, you are dead. You might as well learn right now that *you* are the one and only most important person in your life! You are the one who is keeping you alive. You are the one who punishes you and gives to you. You are the one who takes care of you. You have been entrusted with the care and the keeping of the Christ. How have you done? How have you responded to this parental task? Have you been good to Christ? Have you taken care of God? God is in you, how do you treat what is in you? How do you care for what is in you? Do you love you and all that you are or are you a bully with you?

You are not in this to add more guilt. You are simply in this so that you might "wake up." There are the more obvious ways in which you don't care about you and try to destroy you. You all talk about your health and self-destruction, but do you realize how true "self-destruction" is? Do you realize how much hate against the self is involved before you actually take action and begin to poison the self with various chemicals and toxins? You think you do it because you have always done it. This is not true.

You did not always poison your bodies so. You are the drug and alcohol and cigarette and marijuana generation. You have been linked to chemicals and drugs by your technology. You are part of a cycle and this cycle is self-destruction. Your self-destruction is projected out and made visible all around you. "Everyone is killing everyone" is simply a reflection of what you are doing to you. If everyone began to love the "self," you would see everyone loving everyone else. It all starts within and moves out. You are the projector and you are projecting just what you carry. If you want to see peace and love and harmony in your world, you must begin to show peace, love and consideration for yourself in order to receive your own harmony.

So; how do we get peace, love and harmony within? We begin to look for areas of stress and anxiety in our lives. Then we focus more closely on these tension areas and we begin to ask ourselves questions. We might ask what we are really afraid of, or we might ask how we have been hurt in this area before. You can usually arrive at many conclusions since there are many ways in which you have decided you were victimized or done wrong.

Once you begin to see all of your hurt places, you can tell them how you are now changing and will no longer be creating pain. Some parts will believe you and some will not. You see, these parts have lived in you for many lifetimes in some cases, and each time you come into a new body and unpack your debris from the distant past, these parts have been part of that debris. They know you, and they know how little you have thought of you and how low you place yourself on your scale of important things in your life. You rarely hear someone say how they want to win the lottery so they can stay at home and be with themselves and learn to love themselves. No, you all want to win the lottery so you can throw big parties, buy new cars, and travel.

No one thinks about the self beyond good looks and plastic surgery or a new hairdo. It's not that you aren't aware that you live in you.... Or is it? Do you know that *you* are actually in this body? Do you know that the you that is in this body is God? What a wonderful way to live. God gets to live in you. Aren't you glad you have time to heal you and to take good care of you? Aren't you glad you are still able to receive this information so that you can begin to change – or do you care? Does it not matter to you that God, the creator of all, is in you, or do you just intend to continue with your vices as you always have?

You scream and yell for help even in the midst of your self-destruction. Between your judgments and your damning thoughts and the pollution you put in you, you are actually screaming to God for help. You are so messed up and you do not recognize that you are. You are tearing you apart and beating you up on the inside as well as the outside. Your inner illness is just a symptom of this, and your accidents are no accidents. You hate you and you are punishing you with pain.

Pain will end and you will stop this victim/villain game and begin to love you. Why does it matter? Actually, it does not. You make it matter or not. It is up to you. You create your reality and you get to live in whatever or whichever reality you create. Most of you are screaming for peace so I am showing you a way out of battle. You decide how much or how little peace you want. As always it is your free will choice.

※

When you begin to realize how you are the creator of everything you see, you will understand the gift in this. You will begin to see how you can change perspective at any given moment and, therefore, change how you see or perceive any given situation. You will begin to know how you are in charge of change in your life. You will begin to see how you can create from a belief in abundance and let go of your belief in lack. You are not only the one who creates; you are also the one who receives what is created.

As you learn to live with your ability to create, you will wish to ask yourself how you want your life to be. If you want to know love you must ask for it. If you want to know peace you must ask for it. If you are convinced that you are creator you will want to ask for what is best for spirit. If you do not wish to request what is best for spirit you may want to request what is best for you; for your growth and development.

Most of you believe in giving yourself material gifts and you forget all about the value of supernatural gifts. As you begin to request gifts that are non-observable you will begin to understand the value of them. You actually want and crave physical gifts because you are out of balance in some way. If you want money desperately, it is only because you are insecure and require something to make you feel a little more secure. Insecurity comes from fear, so a good request would be to ask for love. Now; if you begin to feel loved and lovable, you lose your insecurities and the money is not so desperately necessary. You may begin to love yourself and void this need altogether. Money will no longer control your life and be such an issue.

You may also ask for peace. Peace of mind is a good place to start. You require peace because you are at odds within yourself. If you can end the battle within and get all parts of you to like you, you will learn to be flexible enough in any situation to stay calm. Calmness leads to peace. Inner peace is a source of great calm and reserve. This reserve is not so much a holding back as it is a "knowing" that you are the creator. As you learn to be more sincere in your request for peace or love, you will begin to see results in these two areas of your life. You will begin to receive in ways that you never realized could be a gift. You have so many ways to give to yourself that you are unaware of.

You may find that you actually enjoy "creating" love and peace for yourself. You may want to focus all of your extra time on receiving and becoming love and peace. If you can allow yourself to be your own creator, you will find how you get better at it as you go. Your focus will guide your thoughts. Your thoughts have power and your thoughts have the ability to re-create you. You are your thoughts and you are your beliefs. Change your thoughts and change your beliefs.

Once you learn how to manifest what you want, be wise about what you ask for. Do not waste your creative power or drain your energies. Go for what will create more of itself for you. You create from thought and you also create from emotional impact. The greater your emotional impact on any given thought, the greater your ability to create that thought in the material world. You may find that you lose track of your thoughts and do not remember when or why you created specific events in your life. You are disappointed now with your life because it was created primarily by unconscious, or even subconscious, thoughts. You do not know how you really think and feel about life because you are not yet aware of "your self." You do not know you. You do not communicate with you.

You will find that as you grow in your conscious creative abilities you will truly begin to enjoy the role of creator. You will also enjoy being the receiver of your gifts instead of the victim of unconscious thoughts. When you can let go of your need for specifics such as a new bike or car, a new doll or washing machine, you will begin to see the benefits of asking for love. If you ask for love you will open many doors that all work for you. Instead of the new car you may find another way to get around, or you may develop a new way to deal with your old car. Instead of a new washing machine you may find someone who will take care of all your laundry problems for you. You never know what you will create, and once you create it you must learn to receive it. The greatest problem is getting "unlocked," or "moved," out of your mindsets that trap you to one idea or one way of looking at things.

As you learn to grow and to expand your base of ideas about what may be considered good, you will see how you can expand in any given situation – no matter what the situation is. I know you can't see that now, and it feels awful to you to give up "things" or "stuff" or "the material world," but when you begin to let go of the material world you will move into the spiritual world. Spirituality will allow you freedom. This freedom is the freedom to have without owning, and it is the freedom to move from one thing to another without getting "locked in" or "hooked to" your created matter. This was the fall. You fell into matter or the material world and could not get out. You are stuck in the material world. Fear put you there and fear is keeping you there. Your fear of not having keeps you holding tightly to this material world and its ways.

There is a saying "what you desire is what you get." When you begin to "desire" God over the material stuff you will get God. You will have asked for you! You will have put you above "stuff." You will become more important than having things and owning things. The funny part is that when you have "you," you have "love." When you have love you can have everything in creation and you won't really care all that much, so you won't be "stuck" or "attached" to it. When you have "love" you have all that you require and your needs, wants and fears will all vanish. This is what you are moving towards, and this is the "shift" that is taking place now. You are becoming you by becoming love. God is arriving in you.

You are being transformed back into your true self. You are taking off the Halloween costume, and you are coming back home to get on with your spiritual life.

～※～

As you begin to feel your way around and through yourself, you will become aware of your feelings. You have feelings attached to beliefs. Some of these beliefs and feelings were formed at a very early age. You decided that a particular situation must automatically mean this or that. You then felt good or bad or indifferent about that particular situation. Now, as an adult, you create situations to show you how you can choose to see everything differently. You don't have to stay stuck in your old stubborn beliefs and ways of viewing and dealing with life.

Now you see why certain situations never seem to change for you. You are stuck in one way of doing or seeing things. You are afraid to let go and change how you react or respond to certain situations. In some cases you are afraid of your own feelings, so you carefully guard them and protect yourself from feeling them. You once had many feelings and perceptions that freely roamed around in you. Now you block feelings and perceptions out of a fear that you might do something wrong, or something painful.

You are now learning to unblock you and to learn to see you with the eyes of love. Love does not prejudge a situation and love does not condemn. You decide from your fear what is good or bad for you. You decide how to shut down or open up based on your fear and on how far you can be stretched. What is it that stretches you and gets you out of your old ways of hiding from your feelings? It is the will to change and the will to be healthy. There is no one who will force you to change if you do not wish to. If your desire for wholeness and well-being is great you will automatically be drawn to change. It is actually very simple. If you are unhappy and unhealthy try something new. If you are happy and healthy, stay where you are. You will know happiness by your level of pure joy and peace. If you do not experience joy and peace, you are not in a state of happiness. If you do not experience health and well-being, you are not peaceful.

You will find that as you begin to move into some of your old, blocked feelings, you will actually feel sick or even afraid and nervous. These feelings are so shut down and separated from you that you may find them hard to digest. This could create some difficulty in you, and you may find yourself having a very tough time adjusting to your own awakening. It's sort of like puberty is for a pre-teen. You find yourself running crazy with emotions and chemistry that is out of control. This will settle down once you have uncovered and released your emotional blocks. As this process goes on, you will be up and down and all over the place. You will not find it necessary to punish you for being so out of control. This is part of letting go of control and allowing love to take over.

As you decide to change and to move into new and, for you, uncharted areas, you will begin to expand your personality or who you are. You are growing. You are moving forward and you are moving into "all of you" at the same time. You are becoming a conscious being and you are learning to be whole. As you learn to be whole, you will see how you have not accepted parts of your own self, be those parts un-acceptable behavior or un-acceptable thoughts or un-acceptable feelings, it is all part of you that you do not wish to own. This entire series of books is set up to get you into you and into all of you. You will find that thought is energy, and your thoughts can be guided to go into certain areas with new awareness and insight. You can learn to see things from a new, or higher, perspective and then be guided into your darkest, or most closed off, parts with this new information or awareness.

You are stunted and afraid and hiding from the light because you have so much fear in you. Your belief in evil or being a bad person has led you to fear being bad or evil. If something occurs in your life that might look to you like a bad thing, because some part of you once decided "this is bad," you will push that thing away automatically. It could be a "gift," but you think it is bad so you shut off to it. You do not know how to receive and you do not know how to stop punishing you. This is part of how you stop you from receiving any and all gifts that might come to you. You destroy your good by calling it bad.

As you learn to work within love, you will find that you are not so quick to judge everyone and everything. You will begin to see how you are being guided to face all parts of you, and you are being guided to recognize you and how you operate. Self-awareness is self-enlightenment. Self-enlightenment is the self lighting up to rise up. As you light up, the dark places are exposed. Do not be afraid of what you have labeled dark or bad. It is not. You are love and God. It is love and God. All parts of you are love and God, even the parts that you do not at this time accept. You will though. You will accept all of you for you are headed in that direction now. You have turned away from separation and fragmentation, and you are moving towards this. How wonderful you will feel once you have un-trapped and accepted all parts of you.

※

You can find that you do not like you and you can be afraid to discover such information. When you first learn how you hate parts of you, you may have a big part of you who is terrified to know this truth. That big part may not be on a conscious level, and so you may find yet another healing taking place deep within you. When these healings take place you are put in a position of observer. You know how you feel and yet you cannot seem to control how you feel. Feelings are coming into balance and this requires that you allow them to "move."

For a feeling to move it must first be un-lodged from its current stuck position. An un-lodging is usually done by creating an event that is directly in opposition to that particular feeling. The feeling is then sparked and activated and you are put in your place; rather the feeling is put in its place. It is "pushed" toward its proper destination and it is "moved" in this way. Most often you will require movement of feelings. The greatest problem with this healing process is that you hate your feelings! You hate to feel out of control, or angry, or sad, or depressed, or inferior, or less than another. Yet these are all feelings of lack that must be moved. The easiest way to move a feeling is to go into it and move it by being aware of it. You are doing just that when you clear and release. Clearing is a big part of healing. You must clear out the confusion and pain in order to have peace and joy.

As you learn how to accept this path to healing, you will not be so hard on yourself. You will begin to understand how you are organic and how you move with nature. You will begin to see how you are a living, breathing organism and how you affect other organisms as well as the whole of nature. As you learn to "be" and to allow yourself this versatility, you will find joy in being who and what you are. The first step is to uncover you. The second step is to not fight who you are, and the final step is to accept who you are. In the acceptance of you comes the love of you. You will be allowed (by you) to love you once you can accept you. You accept you after you learn to know you and to see you for who and what you are. This is all a process of natural healing. It is a process that involves one step at a time. You are into instant fixes and instant gratification and so you do not have the patience to be you.

Sit back, relax and "be." You are going to come out of this process as an enlightened being. You are turning on the light in you. You are beginning the new, evolutionary process of ascension. You will be so different once you complete this healing process that you will be in "awe" and "wonder" of your own creative abilities. Life will be so good once you uncover and love you!

As you begin to heal, you will automatically come into balance. You will find that you no longer need to be in a state of pain to keep you on your toes. You will find that pain is not your only motivator and that you are not in good condition when you inflict pain on you. You will begin to see how pain has caused you to hide even deeper in yourself and how pain might never have come to the surface without 'intent to heal.' As you learn to deal with your own personal pain, be it physical, mental, or emotional, you will begin to recognize how you are evolving out of pain and into something a little more balanced. Pain is one-sided and it keeps you afraid and down. The opposite of pain is pleasure and you have begun to use pleasure to receive pain. How? You were taught to not touch you. As a child you may have touched you to bring pleasure to yourself. Now you have so much guilt and judgment around masturbation and self stimulation, which originally was pleasure, that now you have guilt, remorse and pain (emotional pain) when you experience self-love or self-sex. As you learn to let go of this need to punish you, you will let go of this game of turning everything good into everything bad.

As you go into you, and as you experience the part of you who is angry and hurt from constantly being put down and condemned, you will begin to reacquaint yourself with your own natural ability to bring pleasure instead of pain into your life. You will begin to let go of shame and guilt and, therefore, you will be free to experience pleasure once again. Sexual pleasure is not your only battlefield of ignorance, but it is a big one and it is unhealed in all of you. It takes a great deal of sexual guilt to create a disease like AIDS. This did not occur overnight. It is sexual guilt being handed down from generation to generation. When you begin to see how you are simply allowing all condemnation to surface so that it might leave you, you may want to have a little more patience with yourself instead of judging yourself more. You are not doing something wrong. You are moving to the light, and you are bringing your unhealed places forward to expose them to the light. This is good!

As you learn to allow yourself to experience what you must in order to heal, you will begin to find feeling coming back to parts of you that once were un-sensitive and had no feeling. You will begin to see how you are not only coming alive, you are also coming awake. You have been numbed by pain and by exposure to pain. You cannot feel for certain parts of you because your feelings are cut off from your heart. You cut them off because you thought it might protect you to no longer feel the pain. Now you think you are painless or pain-free when, in actuality, you are shut down and tuned off to feelings.

This will all change. You are going to get in touch with you and with your feelings. You don't want to "feel" because you think it will hurt. In some cases it may still hurt. Your pain is deep. Please begin to allow feelings to move. For your sake it is best to allow these painful feelings to come to the surface. You will not die from the feelings but you may wish to die when you feel them. To go through your pain is to touch your core. Pain is at the core of your beingness and it must come up and out.

Do not be afraid of feeling – no matter what it is that you are feeling. Own your own self by owning your feelings. You have pushed them down for so long, and you have tried to stifle them and smother them but it only made them angry. You put food in to stuff them down and numb them. You put drugs in to shut them up. You smoke, you eat, you drink, you shut down and you turn off. This does you no good. Begin to allow your feelings to live. Stop killing your feelings. You are killing you each time that you do.

As you learn to grow and to become whole you will begin to see how your feelings have always influenced your life. Now that they are beginning to move in certain areas of you, your life will begin to move in certain areas also. How can you move and become flexible if your feelings are hardened or shut off? A hard feeling produces a hard life. You are guided by feelings and you are moved by your feelings. Feelings can move you to joy or to sorrow. Feelings can bring you up or put you down. Feelings are probably one of the strongest elements of creation. You are allowed to project your feelings out onto others, and you are allowed to share feelings with others. You are even allowed to be free and void of feelings by turning them off.

Feelings are very flexible when they are operating correctly. You will find that feelings allow you to rise up for any given situation and feelings assist you in hiding parts of you who are feeling afraid. You are either part of your feelings or you are not. You either touch them or you are severed and separated from them. Most of you, in an attempt to become mature, have separated from your own feelings. This split within you is part of what is tearing you apart and confusing you. It is amazing how many of you do not realize how you "feel" or have shut down your "feelings" to the extent that you do not feel. You are afraid to hurt and feel pain, so you shut it off. If pain is emotional you will be shutting off your emotional self or the emotional body. This is a big split. You now run on two wheels. Your mental and physical body kick-in to assist. They try to pick up the slack for the now split-off emotional body.

As you learn to heal this split you will be taking a giant step in the healing of you. You will be bringing back a big chunk or part of you. You will become whole and you will end your own separation of self. You will no longer feel so separated and isolated from the "self." You will connect with you once again and you will be whole.

As you learn to get in touch with your feelings you will begin to experience feelings. It may start with sorrow since you have had *loss* of feelings for so long. Mourning may be involved since any loss creates mourning and a feeling of loss. Once you begin to reconnect with your feelings, you may also experience the rage and anger that comes with any split. There is usually resentment and hurt feelings. Be prepared to "feel" them.

Once the initial phase of turning your feelings back on is complete, you will actually begin to feel relieved and even pleased. Once your pleasure takes hold, you may create more pleasure simply by acknowledging it and allowing it to stay and take root in you. As you begin to feel pleasure you will feel balance. Balance comes with pleasure. You have been out of balance and in pain for so long that you do not know how to feel pleasure and be in balance. This will all come to you as you allow yourself to change and to grow. You are learning a great deal about you and your focus is on you. This creates greater stimulation within you, which in turn creates greater movement in you.

Movement in you creates all that static that surrounds you known as your aura or your energy field. You will begin to emanate energy depicting what you are shedding or releasing. This will in turn draw, or attract to you, what you are projecting.

Do not worry about what you create in these days of clearing and healing the soul. You will reflect what you are digging up in you, but that does not mean that it is staying. You are clearing it and so you project it onto your outer world or what you call reality. It is just the debris being set free, and it will allow you to project something more balanced later on.

So; begin to know you and to heal your split and fragmented self by allowing you to be "in" you. Allow you to get in touch with you and to know you. Talk to you and learn who you are and what you do or do not like. Talk to you and learn to listen as well. Ask questions and wait for answers. If you cannot communicate and touch you by telepathy or voice, try writing. The written word is quite powerful as you know.

You will find that writing to you, and communicating in such a fashion, can give you great insight as to where you are and how much you have yet to clear. Basically it will give you insight into how deep within you 'you' might be. Are you buried in you, or are you traveling and moving in you? If you are buried, I suggest you find a way to get yourself unstuck and moving. You can move you in many ways. Ask your "self" how to best do this and then, of course, it becomes necessary to believe the "self" and not be afraid to follow the "self."

As you learn to interpret your feelings and to allow them to be felt, you will find yourself "in" your feelings. Where your focus goes, you go. Your attention on you puts you "in" you. You may find that if you project your focus or attention outside of you, you will begin to feel like you are out of control. The easiest way to calm you and to keep you focused is to put you, or project you, on yourself or in yourself. The more you can focus on the self the greater your ability to heal. You are energy and your energy runs through you. When you focus on you, you create more energy in you.

You are learning now to grow within your own creative wisdom, and this growth is not only intellectual it is also spiritual. Your body is learning to function from within the thoughts you are creating. If your thoughts expand, you then have the capability to expand body. Body is connected to thought and you are connected to all of you. You are the part of you who is becoming aware of the rest of you. You are the part of you who is learning to accept the rest of you. You may discover that the rest of you is actually watching and learning from you. You may discover that the rest of you is actually part of this you, and whatever this you does is emulated by the rest of you.

You are you and you are leading all of you in a new direction. You are beginning to change you one part at a time. This takes a great deal of patience and love for one's self. How can you possibly heal you without first possessing love for you? You will teach you to open to love and to be free of fear. You were always meant to be "in love" and to stay in love with you. You need not buy into the idea that you are unlovable. Begin to teach yourself how lovable you are. Begin to see how you are learning to love the self by dispelling the fears that block your love from flowing. If you believe you are bad begin to change your belief. If you believe you are ugly begin to change your belief. If you believe you do not deserve to be put first begin to change that belief.

You are the one who is in charge of your input now. You are the one who chooses what you watch, read and listen to. You are the one who can pick up a pen and write one hundred times each morning (and night) your affirmations and positive programming. You are the one who will care enough about you to save you. No one else lives "in" you, so no one else can affect your life like you can. You are in control of what goes into you. You are in charge of the care and the keeping of you. If you dented and scraped your brand new car as much as you do your own body, you would be very upset. With your body you don't care. Why don't you care? Because long ago you were taught to care for material things, and it is only now that you are learning to care for you.

As you go along in life I wish you to remember that everything you see is passing and fleeting. Your body does not leave you until the end of your life. Your body is not passing nor is it fleeting during your life. Your body is all you have. You do not own anything here except your body. The one thing you own is the one thing you most abuse. The abuse of you must end. Do you see others being mentally, emotionally and physically abused? Look into your mirror my child. It is you looking at what you do. As you learn to treat you with care, comfort and respect, you will no longer be kicking you around. This will allow the parts of you, who had been separating from you in an attempt to get away from such a bully, to relax and begin to see a whole new side of you. This in turn will allow you to see a whole new side of you.

As you learn to loosen-up and to lighten-up, your entire life will become lighter and less restrictive and less of a burden. You will soon put down this burden of guilt for past sins and you will be free of self punishment. You will learn to release addictions and to free yourself of abusive patterns. You are opening you to receive light, and light will assist in dissipating the darkness you carry. This is a process of transformation and it is different for everyone. Do not try to save your loved one unless you want to live in your loved one. If you want to live in you then I suggest you focus on you, and stop focusing on how much work everyone else needs. Your ability to see how much work anyone else needs is directly connected to the amount of work that you require... yes, another mirror!

As you move from one place within you to another, you are actually viewing you and shedding light on you and your parts. You are so vast that you may not realize when you are looking at you. You are looking at you whenever you see anything in anyone and recognize it. You cannot recognize that which you do not carry. Once you begin to recognize that which you carry by seeing it in others, you will be healing you just by acknowledging your acceptance of what you recognize. Sometimes it is not about hating or judging what you see. Most of you see things in others that drive you crazy, and the thought that this same trait may be alive and well in you sets you off. What you need to start looking at is why it sets you off, not why it exists in you. You don't need to get rid of everything. Some things are actually meant to assist you even though you hate them.

As you go into you and begin to heal greater areas, you will not be so quick to judge parts of you (and others) as bad. You will begin to give you a rest and stop beating you up verbally and mentally. This will allow you to cease being your own villain or enemy. As you let go of this need to judge anything and everything, you will begin to let go of your need to punish you for anything and everything. When you let go of your need to punish you for everything and anything, you will be allowing you to live and to make mistakes without being punished. This allows you to be free of judgment as well as punishment. Can you imagine how good it will feel to stop punishing you? Can you imagine the love you can share when you no longer must be concerned with punishment? Can you imagine how you will be free when you no longer must guard against mistakes? Can you imagine how good you will feel when you are no longer holding part of you prisoner?

You are about to learn to be free, and you are about to learn how to enjoy freedom and to love you for being the one to set you free. You are about to overcome your own programming and to learn to live without the old rules. You are about to let go of the part of you who has played God over you; not a loving, forgiving God, but a false god. This God was a tyrant and this God did not love. This God was control and power hungry, and this God was not giving. He took and he punished, and he twisted what you believed and used it against you.

This God was actually your own ego gone out of control. Your need to be forgiven became so great that your ego volunteered to become a god, so he might assist you in forgiving you. Ego does not know how to forgive because you never taught him. He only knows how to be right. So he became what he knew best and tried to make that work for you. Now he is being replaced as top dog or king within. He is becoming what he was meant to be. He is becoming the part of you who will balance you; not from the standpoint of what is right or wrong, but from the standpoint of what is conducive to your particular life. He will assist instead of fight you at every turn. You are letting go of your ego so you might know peace. In the letting go of your need to be right you will open a space to be filled.

You may fill this space with anything. You may want to fill this space with self-love and the need to be self-love.

As you go about your day I want you to remember to be gentle with you. You are opening to love by being gentle with you. When you do not like you, you push you around and even hurt you. Be gentle and loving, and the part of you who is gentle and loving will begin to grow.

As long as you believe in evil and wrong and bad, you will see evil and wrong and bad. When you can begin to let go of your need to create such scapegoats, you will begin to take full responsibility for all of your own creations. When you do this, you will begin to change how you create. You may deny that you create your own reality and continue to make someone else the fall guy, or you may begin to accept that you create it all and, by so doing, accept that you are co-creator with God.

As you learn to walk down your chosen path, you will learn to be you and to stop pretending that you are simply a victim of God and creation. You will stop feeling sorry for yourself and roll up your sleeves and go to work understanding yourself a little better. You will gain this insight and understanding by learning about you. You will learn about you by observing, accepting and communicating with the self. You will begin to see yourself for who you are rather than observe everything around you and assume that this is who you are. You are not the situations you project. You are, however, the one who projects said situations. I would suggest that you begin to ask yourself why you create what you create. Your answers may surprise you.

As you learn to understand your "self," I would suggest you not blame or judge your "self." You are already carrying so much guilt that your shoulders are sagging under its load. You will wish to lighten your load of guilt by forgiving your "self" for every little thing that you *believe* was done wrong to you. Since you create it all, you will simply be forgiving yourself for what you have created. This type of forgiveness goes a long way in healing the split, or separation, between body and spirit. You may find that you can heal your split by allowing both to communicate with each other. Spirit may require conversation with body as well as with "you" – the conscious you who is reading this book. Once you have healed this split you will find that it no longer tears you apart. The stretching and pulling and struggle for power will cease, and you will find peace within you.

As you begin to realize how many parts of you are at work in you, you will begin to see how complex and vast you are. You will begin to view you in a whole new light, and you will begin to see how great you truly are. As you see greater rewards in this process of retrieving your own soul, you will begin to feel better about living in you and being you. As you feel better about being you, you will be healing and calming and pacifying your own fears. In the pacifying and calming of your fears comes the wisdom that your fears are not all powerful nor are they omnipotent. You may begin to replace your fear with love and not even realize that you have done so. You may also begin to see yourself as lovable and not even realize that you have done so. You may even begin to walk in trust and faith and not be aware that you are.

As you learn to turn you "on" to love, and switch "off" your fear, you will begin to make subtle yet definite changes in your life. These changes may be subtle enough for you to accept them and one day you wake up and say, "Oh my, look where I am. How did I do this?" These changes are what will allow you to become all that you are meant to, and they will allow you to be where you are most needed for the next step of this awakening process. Everything will feel like you are losing, only because you are "letting go" of so much baggage. As this process of letting go continues to elude (you) at times, you will find that you actually miss it. Some part of you will know how good it is feeling to "let go," and this part will not want to stop. As you evolve, you will automatically let go and move on without feeling guilty or out of sync. Most of you have been taught to "hold on" and "letting go" is new for you.

When you begin to understand how you function within, you will be able to stop the dysfunctional behavior. You do this by watching all parts of you. Watch how you gather data to convince yourself that any situation is bad or not good. Watch how you begin to judge and prejudge until you hand down a guilty verdict. This is a process of gathering material and then presenting your material as a definite reason for disliking someone or something that occurred.

As you learn to stop playing judge and jury you will begin to set your prey free. Every time you use this system of judgment you take on the role of predator. You begin to create victims out of those you judge. You become what you most hate which is a bully. Stop playing God. You do not realize what God is. You think that God sits and judges everyone as good or bad, and so you play that same role. That is a false god. It is not good and it is not bad. It "is." Life "is." Love "is." When you can accept that everything occurs in perfect order, you will be allowing yourself to move into the flow of creation and out of the jam that you've been stuck in. So far you are doing well at becoming a well-rounded being. Now you are going to stretch into non-judgment. This is a place that is new for you but you will enjoy it.

As you learn how to stop judging and stop labeling, you will begin to see how you are no longer stuck in a negative position. You will begin to move into a positive flow and this will allow you to be a positive thinker. The good news is that when you think positive and flow in positive ways, you begin to see positive things occur. You begin to realize how everything is only how you yourself perceive it to be. You yourself are finally beginning to be yourself. This whole negative scene you are viewing is not yours. You got stuck over on one side of you. You are now moving into the other side of you. You are going from one place in you to a new place in you. You have operated from this one place for so long now that you believe you are only that small negative projection. You are not. You carry negative and positive, and you actually get to choose which you will project. You are not the one who lives in only part of you. You are beginning to spread out and take over "all" of you.

As you learn to recognize the positive, you will begin to search for and find positive reasons for everything. Right now you are stuck in looking for negative reasons for everything. Once you learn to recognize the positive or good, you will be able to do this in any given situation. Always look for the good and focus on as much of it as you can find. Be in a place within you that will allow you to find good in every situation. When you begin to find your good you will know it. It will feel good.

Now; for those who have not forgiven themselves I would suggest you begin in that area. If you hold judgment against the self for wrong-doing, you will create more judgment and more wrong stuff in your life. If you have forgiven you, you will be able to create love and peace in your life and you will know who you are. The forgiving of you, or self, is the number one most important thing that you will do. To forgive is to "let go of." To let go of is to get on with living. You must forgive you. You can tell if you have, or not, by the number of grudges you hold against anyone who has entered your life. If you have a problem with "them" you have a problem with "you." This is your measuring stick. You are directly related to you, and what you feel for or against another is directly related to you. If you can freely accept others and not judge them, you have made it to a place where you can accept you and not judge you. This will tell you how much judgment you hold against the self.

It would be a very good idea to begin to convince yourself that you are lovable and that you are forgiven for everything and anything that you have ever done wrong. Believe me when I say that you have an awful lot of judgment against you. This is how we stop judgment... begin to break it down. Stop yourself when you begin to criticize yourself and others. Thoughts have power as they are energy. You are energy. They become you. Keep your thoughts about you and others clean and loving. By clean I mean free of clogged, painful judgment. Allow others to be and you will be allowing yourself to be. You can only love what you will allow yourself to love. If you are limited right now do not judge you. Begin to allow you to be and to know that you will gradually expand your love base. You are where you are for a reason, so do not judge you even further. Allow you to be and allow everyone else to be. Watch your thoughts. You will know you by allowing your thoughts to express. Be creative and accept whatever comes forward.

You are now moving into a part of you which is more open and more accepting. Do you ever wonder why things don't go your way? It could be that your way is what you are stuck in, and to be free you must be "moved" into a new way of seeing things. This is expansion. This is freeing you of the prison you live in. You limit you to death. You close you in and close you off. You are afraid and so you shut out everything. "Everything" – including love, peace, joy, and harmony. The next time you don't get your way I wish you to celebrate! It means you are getting out of your prison of limitation and you are being set free. You will love freedom once you adapt to it.

When you learn to know your own self you will be able to see how you allow certain situations to control you. You lose your temper and you get all wound up and upset when you are confronted with situations that are most upsetting to you. This is tied into a lack of love for that particular situation as well as a fear of said situation. When you are angry and upset you are usually being triggered by something or someone who frightens you. You fear loosing to this person, or you fear losing energy or space or freedom or privacy or simply stuff; things; material goods.

When you are afraid and upset, you may begin to hate. When you fear loss, you usually begin to hate your situation or you hate the person you are dealing with. This is how most of you begin wars and draw battle lines. You usually want to erase, or evaporate, the hated person or situation. I want you to know that you hate because you are afraid. You are afraid of not being the center of you. You are afraid of losing more of you. You will find that as you begin to heal and regain lost parts of yourself, you will find it easier to get along. Not only will you be set free of your fear you will begin to feel whole, and this will allow you to release the restrictions, or rules, that you now use to judge others by to keep them at a safe distance. You will no longer require your own criticizing and damnation, and so you will stop criticizing and damning others.

As you learn to work outside of the limits you once imposed on yourself and on others, you will find yourself flowing with creation. You will also find that you have no desire to control creation. Creation will begin to move with you and through you and around you with ease. Right now you block creation by stopping its flow. You judge this or that as bad, and then you begin to put all of your energy into stopping whatever this or that is. You waste valuable energy by fighting, struggling, blocking and so on. As you learn to work more actively and consciously with the creative force, you will begin to see how powerful it can be. You will begin to see how you are part of that creative force that you are fighting. Therefore, when you fight, struggle and block it, you are in actuality fighting and struggling and blocking you. You are creating more problems for you by fighting and struggling. I tell you not to fight because it harms you. Not because it is evil or bad. It harms you!

Now; when you begin to flow with this creative force, you actually begin to flow with you. Once you are flowing with you, you come into balance. Once you come into balance, you do not create situations or things that are distasteful to you. You will create only from balance and so you will be allowed to enjoy the majority of your creations.

You are just now learning to face you and to know you. The next step is to know how you work or, in most cases, how you "dysfunction." Once you know what ticks you off or sets you off, you can then ask yourself why? Once you know why, you can begin to flow with whatever is occurring in order to retain balance. Once balance has been maintained, you can deal in a civil and sometimes pleasing manner in any given situation. Most situations require time. Most of you are so upset by life that you will no longer consider giving time to anything. The saying that "Time heals all wounds" is very true. Time also allows you to calm down enough to see more clearly. If you are upset you use intimidation and manipulation, which causes more intimidation and manipulation. If you use kindness and understanding, you will begin to create more kindness and understanding.

Most of you have no problem using kindness and understanding on those who are weaker than you. You do not, however, use kindness and understanding with the more powerful and affluent. You will find that you are not only 'not' being fair; you are also creating a great split. You show love and consideration for the weak and helpless, and you criticize anyone else. You can easily love a child (if it is small enough), but you have a difficult time loving an adult. You can easily love a pet, but not the guy next door or a coworker. You have become afraid and wary of one another, and this is due to your inability at this time to love and accept the self. You must begin to love you. Start wherever you can. Maybe a soak in a warm bath. Maybe a neck massage. Maybe a nap when you're exhausted. Maybe a walk or stroll in the sun. Treat yourself with loving kindness. Romance yourself. Fall in love with yourself.

You will begin to feel as though you are becoming your own best friend once you have dealt with your anger toward yourself. You are not only angry with you, you are also angry with life and with God. For now we will deal with your anger at the self. Once you learn how to become your friend, you will no longer be so angry, and you will find that you easily let go and work within the flow of life. It is very difficult to work within the flow when you are upset with life. You cannot work with something when you have harsh judgments against that same thing. In the same way, it is very hard to work with and create with yourself when you have such harsh judgments against yourself.

As you learn to project good thoughts and feelings toward your own self, you will be allowing you to feel safe.

Once you feel safe, you can build a bridge between the false you and the real you. As you build this bridge, you will take on the role of the false you in order to accept this part of you. Do not judge you for becoming hostile nor for allowing your rage to surface. You all carry darkness and you all need to release this part of you.

Once you have put a lot of energy into your self-love and self-nurturing, you will feel safe enough to release some of your darker places or your bigger fears and demons. You will feel as though you are going backward into your unhealed places, but in actuality you are moving forward. You will feel like you are never going to end this cycle of clearing and releasing, and yet you will know that this must come out in order for you to feel better. You will not want to "feel" your feelings, but it is necessary because these feelings are a part of you that you have tried to shut down. In order to feel all of your good feelings you must unlock that place in you where you hide feelings. That place in you is full of all your bad feelings as well as your good feelings. Once you open that door you may get flooded with negative thoughts, as these thoughts are attached to these bad feelings. Do not fear. You will not go crazy in your mind but you may feel a little crazy.

Once you get all those blocked and trapped feelings out of you, you will begin to see how you have been holding in a lot of poisonous venom all your life. It is the stuff that bad thoughts and feelings are made of. It is the stuff that makes you feel bad instead of good. It is the stuff that kills you. As you release more of this stored up ill will and anger and hatred, you will eventually begin to see how you have always created what you call your bad situations in life just by this toxic stuff that is part of you. If you are a creative being and you create from what is in you, how can you possibly create lasting beauty when you carry such great devastation and ugliness in you? You will begin to let go of low self-esteem by draining the stuff out of you that hates. In the process of draining this poison from you, you may get drained. It is a part of the process of letting go and lightening your load. You have carried the burden of self-hatred for so long that you think it is actually part of your real self. It is not and it must go. You must allow this false part to release. It is time!

As you develop your skill for entering various parts of yourself, you will become more adept at dealing with all parts of you. Each time you see more about yourself and learn more about yourself, you actually open a new door inside yourself that will eventually lead to another healing. Each time you discover new parts of yourself, you are in essence getting to know the self. Self-discovery is an essential part of knowing thy self. Self-discovery is the art of living within the self with awareness of your programming as well as awareness of your spirit. You are developing into a well rounded being, and you are being moved around inside of you in order to take inventory.

How can you know what you have if you do not realize how you carry everything that is you? How can you know how you are being creatively formed if you do not know what is inside of you creating you?

You are going to discover that you do not love you. The more you look at you the more apparent this will become. When you discover that the enemy is within, do not be shocked. I am telling you now so you will know the intensity of the hatred you carry. Many of you have buried your hatred very deep, and it is so painful for you that to touch it for even a moment makes you feel like you are going insane. You may feel like you must run or get away to shut off these painful feelings. When you touch your rage you will be reminded of rampaging bulls and horror stories of out-of-control maniacs.

You are not going to go into your hatred all at once, so you should be safe from becoming an ax murderer. You are, however, going to touch your rage and you are going to feel it when you do. Do not judge you and do not act out on others. When you hit your rage button you will feel like you are in the right and everyone else is stupid or just doesn't understand. You will be tempted to act out on others and tell them off or laugh at them to put them down.

Rage wants to make everyone else the enemy because rage is in you and rage controls your level of hatred. This level of hatred is how you will know yourself. Your false self is made up of pure hatred. The true self is made up of pure love. When the essence of love begins to touch the essence of pure hatred it is bound to dissolve it.

Hatred knows that love does not require it and so hatred will try to destroy love. Your entire life has been a cycle of hatred destroying love and creating your reality from its false self. Now love will enter the doorway and hatred may come at it strong.

Watch your hatred... it does not want you to live. It is against your true essence which is love. This is the battle within. This is the struggle between the light forces and the dark forces. This is the war that will end in the salvation of the self. Love will conquer all. Do not be afraid to enter this part of you. It is you facing you. It is such a false part that it has grown and developed its own way of ruling within you. You are now going to face your worst enemy and you are prepared. You have been led and guided to this place. Do not worry that you cannot do this. The greatest fear is the fear of realizing that you are hated by someone, you know how dangerous that can be. Now you know you have an enemy and you know that this enemy is within. I have told you repeatedly that you fear being you. This is no exaggeration. You are in dreaded fear of discovering this part of yourself. You want to stay calm at all costs. Whenever this part of you puts its head up you push him down so he can't be seen. You meditate and hide out to stay calm.

This is the part of you who controls you and, by so doing, owns you. You feel a tiny bit of rage and it sets you off to the extent that you only want to feel better. You don't want to feel these feelings so you shut them off and push them down. Now is the time to release them. You have the tools. You have the techniques. You know how to beat on a pillow instead of a person. You know how to release rage by screaming in a safe place. This is all built-up energy that has never been touched and it requires release. You will do well to write to yourself in the times when you are clear and tell yourself you will be okay. You may even keep a journal or otherwise communicate with your fear-filled self. You see, when you communicate with other parts of yourself you build a bridge to that part. If you write a note telling you what to expect, and then read that note when you are most upset and in the midst of your storm, you are extending a life line from one part of you to another.

You will find at times of rage that it feels very much like insanity. It will worry you, but I want you to remember that it is only an energy leaving. You actually assist the energy by hitting something or beating on your bed. This allows the energy to drain more quickly out of your body. Screaming also releases a great deal. These are two very good techniques that will assist you so you don't act out on others and hit them or scream at them. You will feel like screaming at the world, but it is actually you wanting to scream at you. Have you given someone a "piece of your mind" lately, or "put them in their place" with a tongue lashing? You are a very good candidate for screaming out loud in your car or some place private. You must learn that everything you do has a direct effect on you, not on others but on you. Stop beating you up by yelling at others and by putting others down. You are not smarter than anyone else. You all have the same mind of God.

As you learn how to be with you, you will be learning how to share with you. You are the one you ultimately share everything with, and you are the one you keep things from. As you learn to share, you will find yourself in a place that is most comfortable for you. To share with yourself is a golden gift. To keep from the self is an automatic offense. The more you can learn to share, the freer you will be to raise your level of consciousness. This is due to the fact that you are being restrictive and limited when you cut you off from your source. When you allow you to be with you, you automatically open to your source. The reentry of you into you is what this is all about. The false self has shut you out. The false self has taken over and does not want you around. The false self is afraid to give up or give in. The false self thinks everything must be controlled. The false self believes it is right. The false self is in charge and you are waiting to enter this realm now.

Once you enter the false self, I do hope you remember that it is not the true you. Do not worry if the energy is strong enough to make you doubt yourself. You are about to move into a part of you that does not love you and does not like you and really wants you dead. Do not allow this false self to ruin you. This false self actually wants you gone because he thinks he is the one true ruler within you. He is not. You are about to face your own worst enemy, and you have actually been part of him all along. You will find that your false self can affect your thinking and discolor situations for you. He can make things look other than what they are. He can cause you to see things that are not really there. He can project thoughts that create problems for you.

Your perspective has always been colored by this part of you, and now you are going to view how this actually works within you. This is the time to become aware and conscious of what you do and how you do it. It is a time to see how you manipulate and control yourself as well as others. You are learning to look at all of your various parts and this is a part of you. This part creates many problems for you, and this part is very big in you. If you have pain in you, it is this part who is at work.

This part is the one who will hold a grudge and seek revenge. This part is the part who makes you angry so you will not be cooperative with others. This part is the part who believes that you are right and others are wrong. This part is the part who allows you to suffer, because this part honestly believes that you will gain relief if you are punished. This part is confused and this part is heavy with pain. This is the place where you store your pain and it may be highly charged. If you believe you are always right and others don't seem to know what they are doing, you are one who is ready to let go of this part of you. You are letting your ego rule instead of your heart. You are creating problems for yourself instead of joy. You are not in you, and the part of you who is "in" is unconscious.

Once you learn how to deal with all parts of you, you will begin to integrate with them. By going into them you can heal them. You are learning about you so that you might learn to be a better you. A better you would love you and a better you would not fight and push at you. You will find that this part of you, who bullies you, is also the part of you who pushes you to do better and to succeed. There is a place for this part. The role, however, must change from bully to lover. You will find that, as you change this final part of you, you will begin to see instant results in your life. You will begin to feel better and your quality of life will change. This part of you who hates you is confused. He feels like he is in charge and a valuable part. After all, he has been in charge all this time and now he must go, or leave his position. He will feel like he is a victim and he will fight to hold his position. Do not push and bully him for it is not how the new you will operate. Allow him to feel whatever he must feel and do not be afraid of his feelings. They will come out in you. All feelings in you are affecting you, even those created by false parts of the self.

As you continue to learn and to grow, you will be allowed to share with all parts of you. Sharing can be fun and sharing can bring great joy. Most of you do not know what sharing is. You give out of guilt or a sense of responsibility, and now you have forgotten the true gift of sharing. Once you remember this part of yourself you will be allowed to share. Sharing includes intimacy which is very difficult for many of you. You do not know how to be intimate because you are shut off from you. How can you share, with another, something that you have no access to?

---

*W*hen you begin to see how we are all in this together you will better understand how others feel. They are just as manipulated and controlled by their programming as you are by yours. Once you learn to understand that everything that everyone says is not thought-out or even planned, you will begin to let go of the idea that they are out to get you. In some cases you do not even know why you did what you did, and they are no different than you are. They are confused because their enemy is hurting and punishing them too.

So, once we get you to face your enemy and to accept all parts of you, you will begin to know how you will heal. You will automatically begin to see things change just by touching the part of you who has been hiding. All things look clearer in the light, and fears that are brought to the light will disappear. Once you shed light on dark fears they shrivel. It is as though you are a child with a monster in your room casting a giant shadow. In the morning you wake up to find it was a very small doll that was caught just right in the moonlight, and on your wall it made a giant shadow. The stuff about you that you are afraid of is doll-size, but the growth of the shadow is king-size. You will face your own shadow and you will be glad that you did so.

As you learn to merge with all parts of you, you will begin to see how this merging, or acceptance, allows you to join forces within the self instead of fighting with the self. You will begin to discover ways to assist yourself, and you will be very grateful to you for taking this time to love and accept you. The more you can understand, the less you will feel the urge to fight with you.

As you learn to develop a rapport with your own self, you will be allowing "all" of you to be free of judgment. When you have achieved this rapport, or sense of balance, you will begin to see a change in your creations. You always emit energy, as energy is what you are. When you are in an ugly mood you create less than beauty. When you are in a good mood you create beauty. It takes time to create! You project out and it manifests. What happens when you are in a good mood one moment and angry the next? Whichever energy is strongest overrides the opposing energy. Did you feel the force of your good mood, or was your bad mood more powerful? Whichever reaches the source of creative forces is the one that will become your reality. The one with the most pressure behind it is the one that goes the farthest and the fastest.

So; this would indicate that maybe it would be a good idea to look at where your pressure points are and at "what makes you blow!" As you learn to know your own triggers you can begin to work with them. This is not to avoid them but to gently defuse them. This is done by avoiding the need to control the situation that pushes your buttons. Try to be in a situation and let your judgment, or view, or perspective of said situation be changed. This is not easy if you are very set in your ways or rigid in your thinking. The idea here is to be flexible in order to feel good all the time. You want to get to the point where you are in your bliss no matter what is around you. This takes flexibility and a certain perspective. The perspective required for bliss is to see everything as good and not judge it automatically as bad. Begin to know how to find the good in everything. Creation has balance. Good lies within everyone and everything.

When you begin to push your own limits by pushing your own trigger buttons, you will see how you are actually taking responsibility for your own feelings. You will more than likely trigger false feelings that are attached to something long ago. You may find that you do not like noise and chaos. This could be attached to a big "fear of losing peace of mind." As you trigger yourself, by putting yourself in a place where there is chaos and loud noise, you will be upset. You will bring back the old hurt of how that fear was first born in you.

So, as you begin to assist yourself (a little at a time, of course) in this fashion you will actually be facing your fear or facing your dark shadow. It is good when you finally see how shadows work and you finally learn how you do not die from fear; you only kill off parts of you, and then you shrivel and shrink until there is no tolerance left in you. You will be happy to learn that your giant shadow (fear) is only a tiny doll caught in the moonlight. You will also be happy when you take the time to work with you on overcoming your personal fears, instead of trying to control everyone and everything around you.

※

When you begin to understand how you are connected to every part of yourself, you will begin to see how all of those parts have a direct effect on you. You may find that it is no longer a good idea to drop off parts or pretend they do not exist. The more you suppress, or try to get rid of parts, the more these parts will be pushing to get recognition. These parts want you to know that they are you. If you constantly push hatred down, it will begin to push back. The trick is to acknowledge your parts and to accept them. This means accepting your rage and violence and arrogance and any other undesirable emotion you have. You can only change what you own. If you refuse to own it how can you change it or heal it?

So; a very difficult part of your healing will be to admit that you are the monster you most fear. Then you must admit that you are only a monster because you judge your parts as big and bad and dangerous. Once you realize how you create your own monsters out of your own beliefs, you will begin to see emotions and feeling as a part of being human. You will let go of your moral judgments, which will allow you to live within you in peace. You will no longer feel the need to judge part of you as bad or evil.

You will give up splitting yourself into equal parts of good and evil. Actually your parts have been less than equal. You no longer see yourself as half good and half bad. Most of you see yourself as mostly bad with a tiny bit of good.

So as you begin to release the pressure to hold down the parts you call bad, you will begin to see these parts emerge in you. Do not be afraid. Your first instinct will be to push them back down, as they have always been considered subversive in you. Now you will see them and you will feel like they are the enemy; they are the ones who make your life unbearable. They are not. They are human feelings and emotions and projection ploys. They must not be pushed away and ignored. Accept these parts of you and learn to love and accept all of you. These parts must come forward in order to heal and this healing is taking place now. Do not be so quick to judge yourself for feeling what you call negative emotions. Ride these emotions until they exhaust themselves. Work with them to allow them to dissipate.

Once you have drained your trenches, you will be free of the excess build up from suppressing these emotions. Every time you push them down in you, they develop more of themselves in order to push through the façade you present. If you push them back down again they will build up and push back. They are not really your enemy, but you believe they are and you are creator. So you have created or developed an enemy who pushes back at you. This is really their way of getting attention. You have this big part of you that you ignore and their job is to make you aware of them. They are your hurt and pain in emotional form. You do not wish to feel your hurt emotions so you push them away. This will change if you are to heal and to become whole. Most of you will heal this part of you a little at a time. You are too afraid of your feelings to feel them all at once. You will spread this out over time and you will be happy to have time as your friend.

You will begin to see the biggest changes come in how you deal with life and how flexible you become. Most of you are rigid because you are afraid. When fear leaves, you will be less rigid and more flexible. So; do not be afraid of your feelings when they come up. If you have an awful day just realize that you spent your day clearing awful feelings. This is good because it is the draining of you. You will empty out all of your excess and build-up, and then you will fall into balance and every part of you will function smoothly and flow with life. This is a very good time for you, but you will not see that until you have seen and felt the benefits of dispersing built-up, pent-up energy. Energy that is pressurized can blow the top off of a mountain. It is like you are taking your top off to let the pressure release. This way you will not blow molten rock and lava all over and scorch the earth and your friends. You will find this type of clearing very good for your psyche and your soul.

As you learn about these unwanted parts of you, you will see how you have split off from the self and now you are being guided back to yourself. Mother God left Father God and now they are rejoining and forming an alliance.

Once you learn to visit other areas within you that have been unknown to you, you will begin to enjoy this adventure within to discover all parts of you. You will find that you no longer fear being in you, and you may even decide to stay. You all have ways of going unconscious in order to escape. These ways vary from personality to personality. Some of you do drugs to numb your feelings so you won't feel. Some smoke cigarettes to numb and kill cells that send signals. Some stuff food in to shut off the feelings temporarily. The feelings don't actually shut off but the digestion process takes all the energy and attention for a brief time. Some of you shut down by mentally turning off. Others have the ability to space-out and leave the body.

Whatever your technique for getting away from you, you each have one and you use it regularly. If you do not like or trust yourself, you are "gone" most of the time. Your period of euphoria after drug use is you leaving body. Euphoria after and during sex is you leaving the body. Euphoria after killing someone or something is common. Euphoria while beating someone to a pulp is common. These are all ways of exiting your bodies so you will not have to feel. It is very common to escape into one's work or "head-trip." It is also common to escape into one's television or a good book. There are many ways for you to not be present to feel what is in you. You have been escaping life since you were born. Why do you get upset about death when all you really want is to escape being human?

Some of you literally become ill to escape situations. You are very complex and very out of touch with yourself. You are all running away from something, and most of you are running away from you and what you feel. You cannot stand to be in you, so you find ways to distract yourself. Why don't you try being alone with yourself and talking to yourself? How would you feel if people were always running away from you and hated being with you? Not such a good feeling is it? This is how you treat you at every turn. You treat you as unwanted and unlovable. You wonder why you have pain in your life. This is a very big reason for it. You hate you and do not want to experience those parts that you hate. If the feeling is disturbing to you, you will find a way to get rid of it, or override it, or push it back down. God forbid you should feel! Even if it is not that awful, you will shut down out of a fear that it may get awful.

You must learn to accept you as lovable. You must learn to see how good you are and how there is a purpose for your feelings. Some of you are so numb from years of practice that you can't bring your feelings to the surface. You just get confused and shut down more.

I want you to begin to feel. Really feel yourself and your body and your mind and your soul. Know yourself and touch yourself. Touch all parts of yourself. Explore yourself and your life and your mind and your soul and your feelings. Don't leave any part of you out. Do not shut down when feelings come up. If you get a headache, go and scream, and allow yourself the time you require to let these feelings surface and release.

You will not die from releasing and feeling your feelings. You will die if you suppress them and continue to stuff them down inside of you. You are already ready to explode. The whole world is having mini explosions daily. Let's not create a giant explosion of unseen emotional revenge and grief and ignorance and confusion. These energies are stifled and will do anything to be set free. You can set them free in you. This will affect others, in that you are connected to them in an organic matter that is touched by everything and everyone. You will be assisting the world by assisting yourself. Do not be afraid to be you or to feel you. To know you is to know God!

When you begin to understand how you are set-up and put-together and created, you will begin to better understand what you call mistakes and bad choices. You have always known everything there is to know; only you do not know that you do know everything. You are so good at hiding things from yourself that you do not know who you are and how and why you are developing.

You are growing and stretching and evolving out of a desire to be more and to know more. You may choose to sit back and not move forward and not learn more, or you may choose to move on and continue to learn and grow. It does not matter. Some of you go one place while others go another direction. Some want to go to the mountains while others prefer the desert or the ocean. You can go as far as you want or you can sit and stagnate if you want. It is your choice. It is up to you as to how much of what is in you, you want to know. It is up to you as to whether or not you ever communicate with yourself. It is up to you as to whether you undo what you have done. It is up to you as to whether or not you begin to unravel you.

It does not matter if you do not wish to unwind and take a peek at who and what you really are. It does not matter if you only wish to sit and vegetate for your entire life. Or maybe you want to watch TV and drink beer and know nothing except baseball scores. It does not matter. Nothing you do changes who and what you are. You may be unconscious to who you are or you may begin to know who you are. Either way you will still be who you are. The only exception is that, as you are learning about you and going within, you are peeling off layers of you. In this way you carry less of a burden, and your quality of life will improve by removing all the pain-creating stuff.

As you learn to allow others to do their own thing and to be whoever they wish to be, you will be allowing yourself to be whoever you wish to be. Once you are in a position to be of service to yourself, you automatically become of service to others. You are all in this together because you are connected by nature. You are "all one." You are all the same. You all lean on one another whether you admit to it or not, and you all learn from one another. As you see how this works you will begin to allow everyone to be exactly who they are. This is a problematic area for you, and you will learn to know you by investigating you and not others. You are very well known for wanting to fix others because you think you know more than others, and you think you are smarter than others. You are not. You are only more messed up, or you would not have this need to interfere and to set others straight.

A need to interfere comes from a need to fix you. Do not project your need to heal, and to know more, onto others. You are not here to fix anyone. You think that helping others means interfering in their ways. It does not. You interfere and pass your judgments and your guilt's onto others. Leave them alone. You are the one who is in need of fixing, and this need is brought to light by your desire to aid or fix others. Do-gooders are usually those who need help within and cannot help themselves, so they spend their lives helping, or trying to assist, in other people's lives and business. If you are this type of a person I suggest you begin to pay more attention to your own self. Look to the self for your answers. You will find that you are the one who needs help if you think someone else does.

As you go along, you will also see how you do not require all the problems you believe you require. You create problems for yourself to keep you "in-line" or following the rules. This keeps you sure of your righteousness and your rules so that you "know what you know." The only problem is that you create it all. You can create a negative or a positive. You can create a truth or a lie. You can create problems for yourself by the way you set up your belief system.

You will find that, as you begin to release big parts of your current belief system, you will feel rather lost and unattached; sort of like someone who has no roots and does not fit in. This is due in part to the extent of rules that you use to feel morally right and safe. Once you lose your rules, you lose that safe feeling of knowing that you are right and others are wrong. It felt good for you to be right, and now you must let go of that position and just "be." This is floating free, but, for you at this time, it will feel like un-stability and lack of footing. You will feel like you do not belong and you have no place to attach yourself. This will be a big letting go of attachment.

You have always lived by "right and wrong," and when you first begin to see how you set up your own rules regarding what is right or wrong, you will begin to realize how you created it all and how you are un-creating it. But what do you do when you un-create a world of beliefs that have kept you safe from your feelings all your life? How can you survive without this lifelong pattern of splitting off and judging? Who will keep you safe and right and in your righteousness, so you can feel confident that you have done the right thing? God will protect you from now on. You will not create false gods for this job. You need not crawl back into your ego so you won't have to feel your vulnerability and other low self-esteem feelings. God is going to work with you now. This is why you are clearing you out. You are making room for God.

As soon as your need to be right leaves you, you will be safer than you have been in all your life. Your 'need to be right' is what harms you and keeps you down. Your 'need to be right' is your fear in action. If you have no fear then you have no 'need to be right.' Your 'need to be right' is directly related to how you feel about yourself. Your need to be the one in the right is your need to be the good one, so you won't be punished for being the bad one. Your need to be the right one is your way of keeping you from hurting you. You always punish you for being wrong or bad or stupid or not right. So now, with no system of right or wrong and no reason to punish you, you will be free to love you and accept you no matter what you do.

So, if you wish to drink beer and watch TV all day I hope you don't punish you for it. Know that you have better ways of taking care of your body than to put alcohol in it, but do not punish you for it. It is not bad and it is not wrong. It is only a choice! You are allowed to do whatever you want with you because you own you. Love you if you can.

As you begin to fill yourself with light, you will begin to see changes in you. As the light fills you the darkness is exposed. As soon as darkness is exposed it is noticed by you. Your unhealed, dark places must heal. You must love all parts of you and this requires *attention* to all parts of you. As you begin to heal, you will be made aware of the problem or "sick part" of you that requires healing. This is not a "good time" for you. You will feel like these are "bad times" but, in actuality, these are the best of times. You are actually focusing on and healing your deepest wounds.

Anyone who has read this entire series has been guided within to look at the self. Focusing attention on the self is focusing energy on the self. Energy is light and light heals. You are being guided into you in order to heal you. You are guided to information which heals you because you are ready to heal. If you begin to heal one wound, you will usually find that you have other wounds connected to it. You will heal all wounds in order to heal all of you. You are taking all of you into the future. No more fragmented souls searching for their missing parts. No more fragmented spirits who cannot find the rest of themselves. You are becoming whole in order to move forward in evolution. You are becoming whole in order to be free of your desperate search for the self.

You have begun to complete your healing. You are all at various levels within the self, and you may find that you heal best at night when you sleep. A great deal goes on in sleep state, so do not judge you if you decide to nap often. You will find that you can often assist this healing process by getting lots of rest. It's just what a doctor would order for a sick patient; lots of bed rest and liquids.

Now; when you begin to take on large doses of light, you will feel discomfort and you will wish to become calm. You are not accustomed to large doses of light and they often magnify your darkness by shedding light on it. They actually can heal instantaneously, and large doses of light can also cause big chunks of you to come out of hiding. If parts of you have been hiding deep within you, you will be, in effect, shining a giant spotlight on the hiding place. This will cause the hidden part to be exposed. This could cause a shame spiral or sickness for you. You see, you make yourself sick by your behavior. In some cases you have so much shame that you have suppressed deep within you, that to bring it to the surface for exposure will make you feel totally out of control and resentful of being exposed.

This is the process that you most fear. You have carefully judged others in order to hide your belief in your own guilt, and now you are facing the fact that you have always believed yourself to be the guilty, awful one. You will not want to face this part of you that you judge as awful, weak and disgusting. It may cause illness to face this part of you. It may also cause resentment and anger at being exposed. Be fair to yourself and forgive yourself. Do not judge you further. Write your affirmations. "I love and forgive myself" is a good place to start. Do not be afraid to face these parts of you. You do not wish to own your dark side. I want you to accept and embrace all parts of you, no matter how nasty, or vulgar, or dirty, or shameful you believe them to be. Love you. Accept "all" of you.

Once you begin to integrate all parts of you, you will begin to see how you have always bullied you and manipulated you in order to control you. You have been hooked on good vs. bad for so long that you literally use it without knowing. You judge and criticize every move you make. You even break down your days into good or bad days, and you break down your choices and your moves: you did a good thing or you did a bad thing. There seems to be no in-between for you. You are two-sided and you have lost your middle. Your middle is what we are opening up now. You will find that you can no longer stay in your left or your right once you open your middle. Your center is where you have been hiding parts of you that need to be free. Once you begin to heal, your center will not be suppressed and you can move freely through that part of you.

You are going to find that you are no longer the one in charge. You always require control, but now is a time to lose control and to live in the light. Once you can allow control to step down, you will be allowing your own self to live in your center. Your control is how you keep certain parts of you hidden. Are you a controller or are you flexible and flowing? The more of you that you are hiding from you and others, the greater your need for control. If you are the kind of person who holds emotions in to control them, you are more than likely unbalanced and hiding something. A person, who is in balance, will never need to watch how they act or respond because they have nothing to keep hidden, or keep under wraps. If you are a carefully controlled individual you are a walking time bomb. Most of you control your emotions to some extent, and yet you are free to express certain emotions. Others of you watch your emotions to the extent that you look happy when you are miserable, and you don't want others to know how you really feel. If you know how to pretend you are feeling great when your world is falling into ruin, you are a master at hiding. You will find that you are very well hidden from yourself as well as from others. You do not know you.

You will also find that if you conceal most of your feelings on a daily basis, you will be concealing you from you on a daily basis. As you unearth you and your true feelings, you will begin to see how you have lived an underground type of existence that is completely unknown to you. You will find that this entire life you live is a sham, just as the sham you put on is a fake representation of who you are. You may find that you fool yourself more than you fool others, and that your ability to show no fear in certain situations is only your ability to hide things from yourself. If you show no fear you may have hidden all your fear deep in you. I know how proud you are of being strong in certain areas of life, but you should know that sometimes your strong points are actually a weakness in disguise. Not everything is as it appears.

You are a master at hiding things; everything from God to the truth is hidden "in" you. You have no idea how you feel or what you contain. That is the first thing to learn here. You have no idea how you feel or what you have in you. Once you are willing to face that fact you can begin to uncover you. You will not always like what you find, but it will be you discovering you for the very first time.

I have told you repeatedly that you do not like you, and you must now learn to accept this and to move on. Once you can accept that you are at war with you, you will then be in a position to end this war that has gone on since the beginning of time. The dark angel and the angel of light are you. You have carried this energy since time began and now you are evolving up and out of war. You are moving into peace, and that will take exposing your game of war that you have hidden from yourself. Once you discover your battlefield, you will be surprised and yet relieved. You do battle every day and you do not know that you do.

<hr>

You are now in a place where you can integrate and become whole and complete. You are beginning to own up to yourself and to accept that you have feelings that you may not like. To have feelings is to be human. Anger is a human feeling. Jealousy is a human feeling. Rage is a human feeling. You are beginning to know you and to see how you create your own reality. You are doing this by seeing how you "project out," or "stifle in," feelings which are then received as with a radio signal. Either you keep your feelings bottled up and you receive them in your cells and they activate in you, or you send them out at others who will either reject them or take them in. This is energy exchange. You usually send good feelings when you are feeling good, and you send bad feelings when you are feeling bad.

You may frighten someone away by sending bad feelings out at them. You may also frighten you away by keeping bad feelings "in" you. You then must retrieve this part of you who has been frightened away. Many of you have fragmented parts that do not wish to return. These parts believe that you are punishing them by your constant suppression of bad feelings.

You must learn to express your bad feelings so that you do not put extra pressure on your cells. This does not mean that you must unload or dump them on someone else. You are clearing and releasing in order to heal and this is a personal experience. Learn how to have a relationship with your emotions without spewing them out at everyone else. Remember, your opinion is just that – "yours." It has nothing to do with fact or fiction; it is simply a reflection of what you carry inside of you.

So; as you begin to get in touch with your bad feelings, avoid the urge to dump your bad feelings on someone else. This is blame and will be felt as blame. You are all looking for someone to blame and now it is time to stop blame. "Everything simply is." No one is to blame for anything. In childhood you are taught to point a finger of blame so you will not get in trouble and be punished for doing something wrong. "I didn't do it" is common childhood talk. You all look for someone to blame so the focus for punishment will shift away from you. This is a way of avoiding owning your own feelings. These are feelings of fear attached to punishment.

Now that you are learning to let go of right and wrong, you will allow punishment issues to surface. Some of these issues have to do with big sins (wrongs) and some have to do with small sins. All were punished in some way. All have feelings of guilt and shame attached. All are "in" you and in your cells. All are part of you. All have been taking up space that belongs to the light. This part of you is the part that was taken hostage by judgment. Once judgment leaves, everything else will follow. You will begin the "shift" from judging to forgiving.

You are all caught up in judging but you quickly forget innocence. You love to find a wrong in everything, but you are bored by finding the right or good. You are afraid to look for good in others because it may cause you to look bad. You view yourself as less than others, and so, if you focus on how good they are, you cause a greater split between you and them. I want you to learn to focus on how good everyone is... even you! I also want you to learn to "shift" your focus from looking for problems to looking for solutions. I want you to know that you are changing and growing, and you are learning to know all of you so that you might accept and love all of you.

As you begin to accept your own parts, you will begin to see how you are indeed becoming more of your own essence. For most of you, you will realize you have had your essence missing and did not realize how short of it you are. You are all parts of you, and you will begin to see how you literally make up God. Once you begin to understand how you are leaving you and returning to you, you will begin to see how you did not ever plan to be fragmented for long. This was just to give you time to heal and grow and adjust in other areas. Once you began to grow in other areas it was time to begin to retrieve the missing parts of you.

You are so vast and so spread out that you no longer feel as you once did. Your feelings have been disconnected and reconnected to new areas of you. In some cases you have literally disconnected you from all feeling. In other areas you have reconnected to things that are not important and do not matter. Your feelings must be rewired in order to accommodate all parts of you. It is not healthy to be disconnected from parts of you. You must hook back up to you so that you might be in charge of creating for "all" of you.

At this moment in time you are mostly involved with only small parts of you. You will eventually hook up to, and be involved with, the vastness that is you. You will begin to see the parts of you come together as a whole, and you will begin to see how you are working together with these parts, instead of against them. At that instant you will end your struggle. The battle within will end and you will no longer look for ways to punish you or to harm you. You will no longer be at odds with you. You will be in a state of grace that will allow you to flow with all parts and to accept all parts. Even creation is part of you and even creation will flow with you. You will no longer struggle at life. You will begin to feel as though you have no problems and you will begin to realize your full potential.

Once you regain your essence you will find your power. Your power lies in "you." You have been lost and scattered and now you are being returned to you. You (the essence and energy that is you) are beginning to return home to God. You are arriving in you as you read this. Energy that has drained out of you all your life is returning to you. You need not require proof of this. You need only know that in becoming aware of missing parts, you automatically focus your attention on said parts. These parts then respond to this focus or attention by being stimulated or touched. Once this energy that is buried or hidden begins to move again, you are literally bringing it to you. You are bringing dead and shut off parts back to life. Some of these parts only played dead so that they might hide and not be hurt. They played for so long that you cannot remember what they are hiding from, but they continue to hide.

It is not by your conscious choice that you have separated and lost parts of you. This was an unconscious reaction to pain and judgment. Now these parts are willing to return because your new programming is saying something new and freeing to them. The old programming running through you said, "I am guilty of sin and I must be punished." The new programming is saying, "Live and let live for there is no sin." This allows you to drop judgment, and your cells will be free to take on other roles. You no longer hunt for parts of you to punish them. Now you send out signals that say, "You are free. We do not judge you. Come back and be free."

You are a giant communicating machine that not only stores information you also send and receive it. It goes out into the world you see, and it goes deep into you to a world you do not see. Every part of you knows how you are constantly sending signals. You are so wrapped up in your daily routines that you do not realize what you actually do and the extent to which you have gone to communicate with parts of you. You did not always know you were a thinking body, and now you are learning that you are much more than just a thinking body.

As you begin to see your own dysfunctional reasoning, you will begin to allow you to come into balance. You have been out of whack because you were pushed out of whack. When you begin to return to your center you may feel uncomfortable, and you may also feel like you will be hurt. Do not be afraid. You are changing how you behave, and your behavioral patterns are set very deep within you. Once you learn how to change you, you will begin to see how you need not stay stuck in only one position. Positionality is not necessarily a good thing. You may find that you need to move and to accept new ways of viewing any given situation. Do not get so stuck in judgment that it takes you over. Once you have learned to let go of your need to judge, you will begin to see the world as something positive instead of negative.

You are always moving and changing in metabolic ways, and now it is time to change and catch up in physical, mental and spiritual ways. As you learn to assimilate new information, you will be learning how to create new physical matter. Thought creates and thought destroys. Thought can build cities and thought can tear down cities. Thought is what holds you in place and thought can move you forward. New thought is good. Keep good, clean, positive thoughts about you flowing through you. This will nourish you and assist you in this time of clearing. As you learn to go beyond your normal range of thought acceptance, I want you to remember that you are "expanding" as well as contracting. You are becoming less clutter while becoming stronger or bigger spiritually. You are letting go of more in order to receive more of something else. That something else is love. You always thought you had to have certain stuff to feel good and to feel loved. Now you are learning to let go of stuff and embrace only love to feel love.

Love is all powerful and love will assist you in letting go of your fear. Love will also bring joy and comfort and peace of mind. Love... self-love... is very, very important. Once you learn how to recognize you in your daily lives, you will be recognizing how you have sabotaged love in a hope to control your reception of pleasure/pain. As you let go of your control of pleasure and pain you will begin to feel as though you might be crazy. Your control over pleasure and pain has been so strong that you may feel unbalanced without this control. The funny thing is that with this control of pleasure and pain you have been very one sided. Now you will slip toward the other side or find a center balance. If you have been stuck on the right side of you for a very long time, it will feel uncomfortable to move towards your center. As a matter of fact, your center will actually feel like the far left because you have lived so far right.

As you learn to move to your center I want you to consider being happy. Consider letting your guard down, and consider allowing some pleasure into your life. Yes, I know you shut out pain and that pleasure is pain in reverse. And yes, I know that you are afraid of pain, and that means you fear its other half which is pleasure. And yes, I know that you have spent your entire life trying so very hard to keep pain pushed away and out of your life, but you want pleasure now and it is part of pain. It does not have to be a blown-out-of-proportion energy. It can be a signal as it was meant to be.

In the beginning pain signaled you so you would take care of yourself. If you fell hard and fractured your wrist, pain would signal so you would know to go easy on that wrist for awhile. If you cut yourself on a sharp rock while climbing and hunting, pain would signal you so you could heal your foot before going further and creating greater damage. Pain was once a friendly helper and can be again. You have turned pain into something feared. Begin to allow pain to be a signal again. You can work together.

※

As you learn to detect your own behavioral patterns, you will begin to feel as though you have always been in the right. What I want you to do is to be able to see you in others. When you see yourself in others, you quickly assess whether or not you care for their behavior. If you turn around and look at yourself, you will find that behavior somewhere in you. This is how you will detect what you do or do not like about you. If you don't like a particular pattern in them, you certainly won't like this same behavior in your own self. Sometimes you will find that you disguise your behavior so you will not detect it. You are very devious when dealing with yourself. This is due to the fact that you are afraid of yourself. You know that you dislike you and so you hide things that you think might get you in trouble.

One of the problems with hiding you from you (the judge) is that you begin to lose track of parts, and now you have huge chunks of you missing. The good news is that these chunks are still in you. The tough part is that you must now bring them out of hiding in order to become whole. Once you are whole you will have no pain, no worry, no fear, no unpleasantness in your thought patterns. You were created to work within a unit of one, or a whole and complete cell. This fragmented cell has big problems seeing things clearly. A whole and complete cell will have everything it needs to see clearly and to evaluate clearly. Confusion will leave once you allow it to. You hold confusion to you by locking parts of you away. Once you can see how you do this you will be on your way to understanding – which is the opposite of being confused.

As you learn to develop and to use more and more of your own potential, you will begin to change and to feel very, very good about yourself. You will begin to see how you no longer require judgment to keep you safe and in place. You are beginning to return to your "natural" state of being, which has nothing what-so-ever to do with judgment. Once you learn to see everything as it is meant to be seen (which is "in balance"), you will become very proud of you. You will begin to admire you and appreciate you and to know how special you are. You will be in the most beautiful relationship you have ever had, and that relationship will be with your own self.

I cannot tell you in words how wonderful you will feel when you begin to love you. Your feelings for your new born baby are small in comparison. Your feelings for a new lover will pale in comparison. Your love of your new home, with all its grandeur, will not feel nearly as important, nor as strong, as this feeling of love running through your body. You will begin to know you and as you do so you will begin to love you. You will accept all parts of you, and in doing so, you will be allowing yourself to accept all parts of others. Discrimination against certain aspects of your own nature will end. Once this occurs, discrimination against anyone or anything that is different will end also. You will no longer see you as bad, and so you will no longer be able to see them as bad. You will have come out the dark ages and into the light.

As you move ahead in your history (and look back), you will see how these have surely been the dark ages, full of mistrust, greed, envy, hate, despair, pain, confusion and ignorance. Once you move ahead a few thousand of your years, you will see how you are part of a struggling civilization that is no more evolved than a caveman in certain ways. You may have learned to use your mind for technology, but you pushed aside certain aspects of your thinking in the process. Now it is time to come out of ignorance and back into intelligence. It is time to open to the light and to come out of darkness. It is time to learn about you instead of about the world around you. You have discovered and uncovered many great things on this planet. Now it is time to discover and uncovered many great things inside of you. The focus is shifting from outer expansion to inner expansion and you *will* feel it strongly!

As you learn to grow into your true self you will begin to release the false self or identity. The false self is based on perception and how it is used. Your true self simply exists out of wisdom and God source. The false self is comprised of beliefs and statements and quotes and judgments. That part of you is a walking judge and jury. That part of you walks through life and determines what is right and good or what is wrong and bad. As you begin to lose this part of you, you may feel great confusion. You have always worked from and depended on your false self. Now this part of you is leaving and you will feel a little lost and out of control without it. The new self is better equipped to go with the flow because the new self has been evolving and taking in new, fresh ideas and information.

As you begin to change and to grow, do not worry about how you will do. You are being guided and you are still in the process of unlayering, or taking off layers of built up programming. Some of this programming was yours at birth, and some was given to you by parents and others around you. All of this programming is just information which has been used in one way or another. Some of it has even been twisted and turned into something that does not resemble the original statement or belief. You have the ability within you to twist and distort things. You also have the ability to untwist and let go of things. This is a time of letting go of and releasing. This is a time of lightening-up and lifting-up. This is a time of knowing by not knowing. This is also a time of 'being' rather than 'doing.'

As you learn how to be, you will learn to love and accept you for simply 'being,' rather than only loving and accepting you for 'doing.' You are programmed very early for achievement, and you learn to "do" well in order to "receive" awards, or raises, or just good grades. When you can learn how to love and accept yourself for just being, you will have given yourself the greatest award of all.

You are now learning to change and to reprogram your own psyche. Once you begin this process, you may run into old programming that does not wish to leave. This old programming may have to do with fear of being punished for not doing things the right way, or it may have to do with fear of losing everything if you lose just once. This old programming may also have to do with fear of not being accepted if you do not achieve success. You have many levels and fears of loss to deal with, so be patient with yourself and do not fear the self. You are actually coming out of your programmed-self into your God-self. You are switching from the man made to the spiritual. You are becoming a messenger of God. You will not understand some of your reasoning and your motives once you let go of right and wrong. God does not use right and wrong, so you will feel confused about some of your choices. They may no longer be conscious decisions, and they may not make sense to the human part of you. Things are changing! Times are changing! You are changing!

*W*hen you begin to accept you for what you are you will actually be very pleased with yourself. You will become comfortable in your own body and you will learn to be all that you have become. Most of you do not realize your full potential, and so you actually see yourselves as less than you truly are. As you begin to expand your awareness, you begin to be aware of all that occurs and to know how it is occurring. You will begin to sense things and to become aware of things that have always been beyond your capacity to know. Now you will begin to know and you will trust that knowingness.

As you learn to feel how you are being led into new areas of your own creative self, you will begin to feel as though you are expanding and taking on greater energy or light. Once you learn to see how you are being put inside of you, you will begin to enjoy this process. Most of you focus all of your attention outside of you, and you do not realize how much can be gained by focusing your attention on the inside.

As you gradually regain lost parts of the self by focusing attention on these parts, you will begin to see how you are no longer lost and how you are actually quite well-off. You are self-contained and only require information in order to function at full capacity. You are made out of creation, and yet you are the maker. You have only to receive information in order to grow to a new level of operation. It is like a computer that sits dormant because no one knows how to operate it. One day someone hits the "on" switch and all kinds of information begins to pour forth. Then you must find your way around in the computer just as you must find your way around in you.

You are being discovered in the same way you would discover the contents of your computer banks. You have stored information and you have stored misinformation. This is a time to begin to clean out your computer banks and to be free of old patterns and handicaps. This is a time of learning to run you efficiently and to streamline your energy flow. You have always expanded energy without conscious awareness. Now you will learn to consciously use your energy.

Here is a hint for those of you who wish to heal. Do not get caught up in controlling energy in order to advance. Learn how to flow with the energy, as this will multiply your source of energy. To control your situations is to stress out and constantly be on-guard. To flow with your situations is to stay calm and enjoy the ride. If you go up – great... if you go down – great. You only need to learn how to let go and flow. Lack of resistance gives you peace of mind and space in which to expand. The source automatically expands and contracts. If you can be wise enough to flow with this breath-in/breath-out belief system, you will be assisting yourself in the natural ebb and flow of your life. It is as natural for creation as breathing is for you. Although many of you have hampered your breathing with toxins and poisons, you still try to get the breath that life requires to live.

Breath and life are synonymous. Do you shut down your breath or do you expand it? This is what we are moving towards. It is a time of free breathing with nothing in the way. It is like taking in God. You will learn to take in God and to live in the presence of God. Do not put God outside of you. You actually have the ability to put or push the creative force out and bring in the destructive force.

So; what destroys tissues, bone and cells? Not God force I assure you. You have created a negative force to eat you up because you have judged you as bad. This force is actually made from God or creation, as all is God, but it is twisted to the opposite end of God. When you go to the opposite of light you get dark. You have been dealing with light and dark for eons, and it is as much a part of your makeup as being holy or being evil. You have an easier time accepting the dark because you have not yet fully been born. It is like a baby who wants to stay in the womb. Sure it's dark in there but it's the only safe, warm place the baby has ever known. And is it really safe, or do the diseased cells of the mother and the father sperm infect and penetrate the unknowing baby?

There is so much to know and so much to learn. You have only just begun to look at yourselves and how you operate. I want you to know that you are not going to end anything by ending your life as you know it here on earth. You only go on and continue this pattern of learning and growing. You may operate at a very slow pace and be stuck in the dark side of evolution for a long time, or you may move quickly into the light and expand yourself.

As you grow in light, you will find it impossible to remain addicted to the dark. You will no longer feel good in the dark, and you will begin to embrace the light. You are moving into the light now, so many of your patterns and addictions are going to fight to hold their ground. You are not fighting with evil. You are simply fighting with you for you. You (part of you) want peace, happiness and love. Another part of you does not believe you are good enough. That is the part that makes you feel bad or uncomfortable enough to slip into addictions.

Once you free yourselves of your addictions and patterns, you will be giving you a break. Can you imagine someone who hates his or her self enough to poison his or her self with drugs? Isn't it amazing that cigarettes and alcohol and drugs are so widely accepted and a comfortable part of your life? You never began to think about such things until recently, and that is only because you hear how many die from killing off body parts. You have such a blasé attitude about destroying body parts... as though it's not your concern. Think about it. Really think about what you do to your body and then think about why.

Are you loving you or are you trying to kill you off a little at a time, and, do you really care? And if you don't who does?

One of the most interesting parts of you becoming you is that you will no longer feel like you are an outsider. You will begin to feel like you are a part of everything, and this will be due to the fact that you have finally accepted all of you. You will find that you no longer feel lonely and you no longer feel as though you have a problem with life. You will begin to feel as though life were created just for you. You have always wanted to be part of creation and only your fear kept you separate from it. Once you enter the flow you will be amazed at how you are being guided and rewarded. You will begin to see how you are not only learning to see the good in all things; you will also begin to recognize how you create all things that you receive.

Once you learn how to create and to receive from consciousness rather than unconsciousness, you will begin to form an alliance with the part of you who does your creating. If you do not recognize that you create everything in your life, how can you become friendly with the part of you who does the creating? If you do not realize how you create everything and then blame God, or life, or your neighbor, how can you begin to change what has been created? If you own that you create it, then you can take steps to be responsible and to change it if you do not like it.

You must begin to realize that there is a part of you who creates and it is not always to punish you. You often create good situations for yourself and you call them bad out of fear. Some situations are actually created for you so that you might grow and begin to recognize your own potential. Many of you do not realize the power you carry and the ability to express that power in creative ways. Do you know that you are one of the most powerful creative forces in this realm? We only need to get you focused on creating and out of your focus on punishing and destruction. Once we can refocus you, you will be fine.

As you move into a consciousness mode and out of the unconscious mode you have been stuck in, you will become clear and you will see how it is no longer necessary to punish you. You will begin to open to the fact that you are no longer bad, or considered bad by those parts of you that believe in judgment. You will begin to feel free and you will begin to feel safe. You have not felt safe in a very long time. This is due to the fact that your enemy is inside of you. Your own belief system is attacking you and punishing you.

As you learn to realize your own good potential, you will allow this old belief system to reprogram. This is when you get to see how great and good and wonderful you are. This is when you get to see how you are God. This is when you get to feel good about yourself. Can you imagine just feeling great about who you are for no reason other than belief? Can you imagine feeling like a giant prize winner or Oscar winner, without having done anything except forgive yourself? Can you imagine walking on air like you just fell madly in love, and the one you are in love with truly loves you in return? Can you imagine if that lover who is making you feel on top of the world is you?

Now; you may begin to wonder when this glorious day will occur and I will tell you now that it has begun –

from the first moment that you decided to heal and to change. Now it is just a matter of how long it will take to reverse programming in you. You must be patient as you release the old and take on the new. You are in the middle of transforming and changing now. You are growing in love and letting go of fear. You are in the process of turning on the light in order to live in the light.

You love living in the light. Your body will thrive and your mind will be at peace. The light is the love you have always searched for. Your own love is what you and all of mankind have sought since time began. Your own love is not elusive; it is right inside of you. You will find it when you dig up your fear. Fear is the opposite side of love and they are buried together in you. You must face your fear in order to face your love. Love and fear are one and the same energy line. It is just how you see it. If you fear someone you do not accept them. If you accept them you love them. You will find that as you dig up your love, it will come to the surface with your fear. Do not worry. This is how you uncover you and dig you out of fear or darkness. You bring it to the surface so you can accept it. Once you learn to accept everything, you will be loving everything. Once you learn to accept you, you will be loving you.

As you go along and dig up fear that is buried, it will probably bring discomfort to you. This is the law of attraction and repulsion. Like attracts like, and so your fear will magnetize more fear to you. This is what occurs when you begin to love you by bringing your fearful parts to the surface. Once all of these fearful parts have surfaced and you have dealt with them, you will be less fear-filled and more love-filled.

As this process continues, you get to see how you are unloading fear by watching and observing it, and you are taking on light by knowing that this is acceptable. What you believe is what you create. You are emptying you of dark fear by knowing or believing that you are. Remember, the stronger the belief, the more powerfully it creates. If you want to go faster, you can speed it up by simply wanting or desiring more light. This is how many of you have accelerated your healing without knowing that you have. If you are having big problems facing and accepting your fear, I suggest you slow down the process by slowing down your desire for a speedy recovery.

Healing takes time, and sometimes it even takes patience on your part. The more time you can give yourself to heal the less "pushed" or "rushed" you will feel. Your patience to you is actually a gift. If you always feel hurried, it is you pushing you. Look at how you push you around – and then stop. Stop bullying you. Do not bully yourself, as it gets you nowhere and it inhibits the natural flow of things. Learn to flow. There is a time for the intake of breath and there is a time for the expulsion of breath. It is as easy as going with the flow. The flow will take you exactly where you need to be. Be at peace, and learn to let go of your desires enough to flow with the natural flow of things.

As you learn to break free of your need to be right in order to be good, you will begin to see the benefits in allowing others to be right. People love to be right because it makes them feel smart and good. How can you be wrong and still feel smart and good? You will learn once we get your programming changed. Once we can get you to give up your fear of punishment, you will no longer feel that to be wrong is a punishable offense. Once you let go of the need to punish yourself, you will no longer draw punishment. Some of you take things away so you won't be happy. Loss upsets you, so you use this process of taking away from the self. If you begin to see this as a gift from God you can no longer use it as a punishment. You can actually reprogram all parts of you and become a completely new person. Once you learn to do this from a conscious level, you will be working with you instead of against you.

You are going to learn to be a new person and you are going to become transformed. You are also going to learn how creation works, which means learning how you work. You are coming into you and you are healing all parts of you by doing so. You have had a giant split running through you for eons, and now you are bringing both sides of you together to become whole. The male/female of you is becoming whole. You are becoming one. You are merging the left with the right. You went as far away from center as you could get and now you are returning. You are not going to fight and argue within you any longer. You are going to become agreeable, and you are going to settle all disputes you have against yourself. Once this takes place you will begin to see your world change. The emphasis will be on good not bad. You will come back to center and not be to the extreme right side of bad. You will bring it back to center where it meets and connects with good.

You will begin to automatically see good in everything. Part of this will be due to the fact that you have taken off your tinted, distorted glasses that you use to view everything. You view the world through your pain and other emotional experiences. Once you change your experiences by allowing them to be acceptable, you then begin to see everything as acceptable. You are headed in this direction. By accepting all parts of you, you will be accepting all parts of your world. Life will change as you see you change. Life will soften and become nonjudgmental as you begin to soften and become nonjudgmental. You will find yourself actually liking yourself, and then you will find yourself actually liking life. Love will begin to seep into all the spaces being vacated by fear, and you will begin to feel love once again. Love of self is the greatest love of all. You contain a universe, so to love you is to love universally. You are universal in your love, you just have never been told before how to reach that part of you.

Once you begin to reach this love that is God force, you will begin to feel very good about yourself. You will feel like you know something that is special and secret.

You will feel like you have been privileged to know you. You will feel like you want to be you and you will feel grateful to you for this wisdom. Once you know you, it is impossible to not love you. You have never truly known you before. You needed a guide into you in order to see how you work.

Once you begin to bring all parts of you into your own awareness you will be conscious of many feelings that you carry. Not all of these feelings are to your liking, but you will learn how there is a purpose for each one. You will also learn why you have suppressed them or shoved them into hiding places within you. Let your feelings out so you can feel good instead of bad. All feelings are attached to good or bad. The bad feelings need to bubble up to the surface in order to release. You also get to view these bad feelings and see if you wish to "hold on" to them for a while longer, or if you are ready to "let go" of them. This is the time to clean out you in order to bring you back to center balance. You will find that once you find center, you will feel much less stress in your life. It takes a great deal of resistance to keep you permanently off-center. Remember: there is never pain without resistance.

※

Once you learn how to operate within your own wisdom and outside of ignorance, you will be seeing remarkable changes in you. You will find that you no longer require excitement, as you will no longer feel bored by life or your world. Once you eliminate the use of excitement, you will begin to calm down and to know peace. In some of you, excitement is in control. Once you reach a certain level of calm and stability in your life, you begin to long for action. You want more, and so some part of you complies by creating something new and stimulating. Usually what is new and stimulating is also a challenge. So now, instead of peace and calm, you are over your head in a stimulating challenge. Once you learn how you create new changes, just by your desire, you will begin to see how you can consciously create and no longer feel like the victim of your creations.

As you move into consciousness, you will begin to realize how you have had a pattern to the way in which you create. You get to know your own pattern and to work within it. Now you can control you and how you desire or create. This will allow you to create differently. As you go along and create your daily reality, you will begin to see how you are being guided by a new part of you. This new part of you has been growing since you became aware of the fact that you are God the Creator. This new part of you is insight, or awareness, and it is taking over for darkness and ignorance.

As your insight and awareness develops, you will begin to turn your attention toward your greater awareness and off your pettiness. Once this has taken place you will no longer think small or be narrow minded. You will be secure in your knowingness, and you will begin to know that you have simply been programmed to be who you now are. Once we reprogram you, you will be a new you with new awareness, which will then create in new ways for you. This is the key. You will be creating for you and no longer against you. You will begin to settle into peace without assuming it to be boredom. You will know how to stop zinging around and throwing your energy.

Now; one of the benefits of living in peace is that you calm down and don't blow off steam so easily. You will have disarmed yourself to the extent that you may no longer be explosive. You may simply be in a state of calm and still think that your life has become boring. It's only you not knowing how to "accept" the simple pleasures of life. So, whenever you feel bored, look to see how you have created this bit of peace and calm. Don't be afraid to not be "in action." You are meant to have balance. This does not mean constant action. There is also inaction. One of the best ways to accept pauses in your life is to realize that everything is in perfect orchestration and everything happens for a reason. When you feel a pause enjoy it, and do not be put off or upset that things don't seem to be moving. Once in a while you receive a brief respite from the excitement and struggle you have created. This is a good thing. Don't be afraid of being bored to death. You will learn to appreciate and even enjoy what you call boredom.

$\mathcal{A}$s you go along, you will begin to see how you are no longer being hurt by you. You hurt your own feelings and you physically hurt your own self, and you even create great illness. You have not been taught to deal correctly with your power. You are the Creator of your world, and no one ever taught you how to deal with that and how to create for yourself in helpful ways. You will learn how to express your creative juices in the most helpful ways, and once you do you will no longer feel the destructiveness you now feel. Once you learn the basics of cause and effect, you will see how every action creates a reaction and how every reaction creates another action. Usually things have a domino effect on you and on others.

Once you begin to see how you create from an energy within you and you begin to see how this energy is not only you, it is all of you, you will begin to take responsibility for all of you by getting to know all of you. As you get to know all of you, you will understand more of your created world. You will see parts of you who panic and lose control, and you will see parts of you who get angry and step forward to take control of the situation. You may even see a part who is trying to mediate and keep you calm.

Most of you will begin to see your original parents in you as well as your own child self. You will see how you have taken on the roles of your parents and maybe even grandparents. As one generation creates another, they automatically create it from themselves and all that they are made of. If thought is living energy and it inhabits every part of you, it would also inhabit your sperm as well as your eggs and ovaries and womb. You are not passing things on to your offspring so much as you are cloning, or creating, "more of you." You are re-creating what you are. Change what you are and you change what you create.

You will find that as you continue to use this process of creation, you will begin to take greater care to know what you are creating. Even in this part of your "powers to create" you have not been correctly informed. You believe it is good to raise children and "pass things on." This would be true if you were even half aware of who you are and what you are passing on. Do you wonder at the rage and desperation in the young people of today? Your creations are going astray because you are unable to give direction to them. No one taught you who you are, so how can they know who they are? Here is my suggestion; stop having babies until you know what and who you are, and this will assist you in cleaning up your messes. It is only a suggestion and I really don't expect you to listen for quite some time. After all, you do what you want because you think you have all the answers. Just as your young do what they want and think they know all the answers.

So; as you learn to grow and to accept that you create it all, you will also learn to take responsibility for it by acknowledging it as "yours." If you want to learn to create wisely, I suggest you begin to allow for the truth, and the truth is that you are not functioning in your best benefit. You are functioning out of fear, and programmed information, and superstition, and ignorance. Wake up! It's time for you to learn and grow in intelligence and come out of the dark ages. In the future you will no longer find it necessary to produce offspring or another part of yourself. You will no longer need to create someone to love you so you won't have to learn how to love your own self. Once you see why you are procreating, you will begin to see that the fulfillment comes from owning someone small who loves you and depends on you. This is natural and yet it is getting to be an addiction with you. You have created many addictions in your search to make you feel better in your life, and this is becoming a big one for the young.

As you learn to no longer fragment and separate the self, you will begin to see how beneficial it can be to remain whole and complete. You are not only 'not' complete you are terribly fragmented. This is the time that you have chosen to come together and become whole. This is also the time that you have chosen to become aware of all that you are. As you learn to heal the wounds and bring together your male and female essence, you will become whole and healed. As you become whole and healed, you will be filled with love and no longer split by hate and revenge. You will begin to see how good you are because you will feel good. When you feel fragmented and split you do not feel good, you feel bad. This is a time of healing the split within you. The division that has been created is being absorbed and healed. You are going to become whole and complete, and you will truly feel fulfilled.

As you begin to move into your own wholeness and specialness, you will find that you are no longer lonely and searching for something, or someone, to fulfill you. What you have always searched for is your own love. With your own love will come forgiveness and self-esteem. Once you can learn to be in your love, without running from it, you will learn to absorb it and to live with it. Love is a stranger to most of you. You do not know how to love, and so you are being put in a position that is new for you. Once you learn to be you and allow the false self to fall away, you will also be part of your own growing, developing self, and you will let go of your old fragmented ways. Now that you are developing and learning to be "one," you will no longer be drawn to separation. You will wish to be all that you are and you will wish to remain you. No more leaving you, and no more abandoning or rejecting you. You will accept you and you will stay with you by staying in you.

As you learn to develop and grow within your own ways and abilities, you will begin to appreciate your ways and to love being you. All that matters is that you accept you and do not fear being you. You must learn to be all of you and to allow all of you to exist. This includes emotions and feelings and even unknown parts. You are the best you can be when you are present in you and present in the moment. When you leave you, you will see how you are no longer being present nor are you being love.

*A*s you continue to delve into the workings of your inner beingness, you will begin to receive credit for your initial search for wholeness. You will begin to feel fulfilled and you will begin to feel complete. It is not so much that you have been incomplete; it is more like you have been absent or missing. Now you are coming back to you. Now you are regaining the parts of you who were pushed away into the corners of you. Nothing is ever a total loss. You don't push away parts of you and they fall into never-never land. You always store these parts somewhere, and this is how you hide you from you. Whatever you once hated about you is stuffed in you and is also trying to release itself so it might have life. You determine what parts of you deserve to stay alive and what parts you will put away to never see the light of day.

As you continue with this process, you will learn to release you so that you are no longer held prisoner by your own rules and your own fears. Once you can break free of your fear you can have anything and you can be anything. As long as you continue to break your own rules and to move and expand, you will be seeing dramatic changes in your outer world or how you "perceive" your outer world. You are now in the process of determining your own growth rate by allowing your rules to fall by the wayside.

Most of these rules are very personal, and you have set them in place to protect yourself and to determine your own rate of growth. As you set your rules, you allow yourself to "hold back" or hold you back from going forward. You get stuck in a rut or stuck in the moment, which then slips into yesterday or "your past."

In order to live fully in yourself and in the moment you must come out of your past or, to put it more correctly, you must come out of your memory banks and into the present. This is what healing is all about. It is about bringing you full circle out of your beginning and into your "now."

You will find that the more you learn to stay in the "now," the easier it is to receive creation and her gifts. You are meant to love and you are meant to receive love. You receive from your source and you give out to your world. If you are light, you need never "give" light because light is not tangible. Light creates and light illuminates. Light does not touch you, you are the light! When you send out illumination, you will begin to see how you are no longer losing your light. To strengthen your ability to illuminate is to become stronger at your source. Your source is God and God is you. "You" are your source. Now; when all parts of you begin to rise up to freedom from rules and fear, all parts of you will be "free" to shine. This allows you to become light with little to no darkness. This allows you to dispel the myths of your programming and to become all that you naturally are.

Once you begin to see your parts shining, you will know that you are integrating quite nicely. As you integrate, you release your hold on darkness for that particular part of you, and that particular part is then set free from the judgment that was originally placed against it. You will then go through a process of struggling to hold on to your old rule that kept the judgment in place to keep the part submerged in you. Once you have let go of trying to hold on to the old rule, you will slip into the present which is "rule free." As you go through this process, you will begin to see how you are actually setting you free so that you might live in joy, which often has been drowned in all that sorrow for stuffed or submerged parts. Your joy is under the surface and moving quickly into balance. You will have joy and joy will know peace of mind.

As you learn to balance in all areas of living, you will begin to see how you have always been taken care of in one way or another. You thought no one was there for you, but you were taken care of by someone. You were taken care of by a source that is greater than you. You were assisted. Liane often cries about how alone and forgotten she was during her abuse. She was not alone. She screamed and screamed (in her own head) for help and she was helped. Parts of her assisted by getting her out of her situation. She was being violated, by earth standards, and so she was pushed out of body so she would not remember her trauma. She was saved from what she had created, in that she was knocked out and drugged by her own body so she would not go insane and lose control of her mental abilities and capabilities. This is how the source protects when it cannot directly intervene. It is not likely that any one of you is outside of this source. It is only a matter of becoming conscious to it, so you might learn to assist it instead of always wanting it to assist you.

As you learn to see how there is a pattern and a plan for you, you will begin to feel how you are a part of something much larger than just what you see. You are part of a source that is so vast you cannot comprehend its greatness. If you will stay calm and stay unafraid you will always be connected consciously, or more consciously than you now are. Now you are stumbling around in the dark instead of "listening" for the sounds that guide you. You do not see the signs posted for you which are actually the events which occur in your life. You will learn to notice when gifts come your way and you will learn to hear the voice that guides you. As you learn to decipher the signals that are put in front of you, you will begin to see how help has always been available if you only know how to see it.

Once you learn to see what you are searching for, your search will end and you will be connected to God. You will be with the universal mind which can signal you of any impending doom. You will no longer deal with fear, you will deal with trust and faith. It is so much easier to deal with trust and faith than it is to deal with fear and panic. So, as you go about your day I want you to learn to be a part of the source by watching for signs to keep you calm. Usually the source will send you signals that say, "This is the direction," or "this is the way to go." Stay calm and reconnect with the source. You are part of the source and you will benefit by reconnecting with this part of your own self.

※

As you discover your various hidden parts, you will begin to know how you are not only being put back together, you are also becoming all that you once were. This is a new beginning. It is the chance for you to start fresh with a whole new you. You can let go of your past and move into the present with ease and with grace. You will find that the more of you who comes back to you, the greater your ability to be whole and in balance.

As you accept your pain and ego and anger, you will be allowing them to come into balance instead of being shoved down into a corner of you. Once you accept all of the undesirable parts that you have always pushed away, you will begin to know who you are. You also begin to know what you are meant to do in any given situation. You no longer have confusion and you instantly "know." You will find that you no longer have difficulty deciding where you should go, or if you should go, or if you should stay. Everything becomes clear and you become the observer. This takes a little time only because you must be in balance which means healing. This is why you are walking this path and healing now. You are not a masochist who enjoys feeling your pain for the sake of pleasure. You are feeling your pain in order to release and ease your pain.

You are giving you the greatest gift of all. That gift is "freedom." You will have freedom from guilt once you drain your guilt. You will have freedom from pain once you drain your pain, and you will have freedom from judgment once you drain your judgment. You are the one who will benefit from the healing work you now experience as pain and discomfort. You are the one who will feel better in the end.

Do not be afraid to touch your pain in order to heal it. In some cases your pain will feel so strong to you that you will no longer believe that you are healing. You will begin to feel as though you are getting sick instead of getting well, and you will begin to feel as though you have gotten nowhere and are wasting your time and energy. This is when some of you will want to stop healing, suppress what is coming up and go back to not knowing and not caring about what is stuck in you. You may stop if you wish. You own you and you get to do whatever you wish with you. You may find life very unrewarding if you do not completely embrace all of you. For how can you embrace all life if one is no longer embracing all of the self? You will learn to know you by looking at you... all parts of you, and you will learn to love you by accepting all parts of you. If you leave some parts hidden, you will not know them and you will not be embracing all of you.

To know you is to be in touch with all of you. There are many parts of you that you are afraid to touch. If you touch them you are afraid they will move. If they move you are afraid they will take over and make you into a monster. You know your capabilities and your level of anger and rage. You know what is hidden in you and how you suppress it, so others will not see this part of you and go running and screaming out of your lives. You really do know what you contain, and you hold it in and pretend that it is not even there. You think if you pretend long enough it will go away. You are mistaken. It will not go away. How can it go away if you are pushing it deep into you? It only becomes a part of you, and the deeper it is pushed the greater a part it becomes. Depth allows it to touch more parts of you and your inner workings.

You want to unlodge and bring to the surface all unwanted garbage. This will allow you to see it as more than just garbage. This will allow you to see how what you suppress, or push into you, will affect you deeply. You must clear out your deeper wounds in order to heal. This is not so much painful as it is confusing and crazy. You will feel the loss of your peace of mind and this loss will feel painful to you.

Do not be afraid my child. You are no longer walking alone. You are being integrated and you are learning to care for your own soul. You are becoming one in body, mind and spirit. You are learning to heal you by knowing you. I realize that you do not want to know all the garbage and pain you carry, but it is a good way to learn who and what you are, which will allow you to accept and love who and what you are. This in turn will allow you to heal who and what you are.

Once healed, you fall into balance and shift gears. You shift into cruise and your life becomes a very pleasant journey. No more pain and no more fear. You will truly, for the first time since incarnating, be happy. You will know joy and pleasure and peace and harmony. You will not have to sit in a meadow to know this peace; you can be in the middle of rush hour traffic on a busy city freeway. You will feel just as comfortable and peaceful as if you were sitting in a quiet meadow. It will be peace within you that creates peace in your world. You are the pioneers of peace. You are the "A" team and you are clearing and making a path to be followed by the next team.

So; know you and eventually you will know peace. It all begins and ends in you. You are the creator of the world that you see. Be blind if you want, or choose to see clearly. It is all up to you, for you have free will. Use it wisely.

When you begin to know how you operate from within, you will no longer blame everyone else for your misfortune or even your fortune. You will begin to know that you are the one who is asking for and receiving all that you receive. You just have to figure out what you are receiving and why you think it is undesirable. When you learn that you create from all parts of you and that those parts are at odds with one another, you begin to see how the creation process might become a tug-of-war.

As you learn to integrate all parts and allow them to be acceptable, they will begin to settle down because they have finally gotten your attention. The deeper suppressed a part may be, the greater it will push at you to be heard. It is time for you to heal, and these unhealed places are certain that they will be forgotten if they do not push forward before you decide to give up healing. They have gone unheard for so long that they are frantic and will do anything to receive attention. Once you have given them attention you will be allowed to connect with them once again. This reconnection will be a reunion of sorts, and it will cause a small discomfort, as you are not accustomed to using this part and it is not accustomed to sharing with you.

So; as you learn to put up with and become accustomed to these unknown parts, you will be learning to share you with you. This is a whole new area for you as you actually have very little patience with you, and you even have some hatred against you. If you begin to feel self-disgust and hatred, it is coming from releasing these buried parts. You actually want to celebrate if you begin to feel these parts move. It is a good thing to move your darkness into the light of day, and it will eventually end the tug-of-war process that goes on within. This will lead to a union with you and your alter ego. You will begin to integrate all that you are and to heal your split.

As this process of integration continues, you may begin to see some big changes in yourself, and you may begin to take life with a grain of salt. You may even catch on to the flow of creation, and learn how to move with it instead of struggling to stay in one spot. As you learn to connect with the flow, you may also learn to be whole. As you flow, you become part of the natural flow, and this leads you to become part of the whole of creation. You will no longer fight against what you naturally are.

When you get to a point where you can easily and readily accept certain parts of you, you will become more of those parts as well as them becoming more of you. This is a melding of you into you. It is a nice blend that takes away any sharp edges and allows you to soften and become calm and peace-filled. As you become peace-filled, you will also become a loving being. It is difficult to not love when you are peace-filled. The lack of love in your life comes from the tug-of-war. When at war how can one see love, even if the love is always there?

So; as you learn to end your tug-of-war, you will be doing both you and your alter ego a favor. You will be healing the split in you. Fragmentation will end, and you will be working from wholeness rather than half consciousness. You "know" without reason and you will "trust" without proof, and you will have faith in you. To have faith in you is to know you are part of something greater and to realize that you are connected to that greatness. This leads you to your awareness of your God connection. This allows you to open to more greatness than you have ever known.

As you continue to walk this path to hope and faith, I wish you well. You are learning to be whole and to retrieve all parts of yourself in order to know all of you and, in doing so, heal all of you. You are coming into consciousness and you are becoming all that you are. You are learning to be God. God is entering all of creation. God had always "been" and always will "be," but you did not realize that God is you and you are God. Now that realization is coming into you and that realization brings with it "consciousness." You are becoming a "conscious God" where once you were an "unconscious God." The only thing that is changing is "you." You are your state of consciousness and you are healing that part of you. You are waking up and you are "feeling" you as you do so.

Do not be afraid to know you, for you have suffered long enough from fearing what you are or might be. You are learning now that you are the glory of God, but no one ever told you who or what a human being is. How can you know if no one told you and you shut down your power to get into a body? The fallen parts of God are simply the parts that went unconscious. They went to sleep. Now they are waking up!

※

You will begin to see how you are programmed to respond in certain ways in any given situation. You also find ways to show your fear and upset without being honest and forthright. Once you learn to spot how you act-out certain behavior, you will become aware of your tendency to act-out. You will find that you are also good at showing how you feel and not so good at expressing verbally how you feel. You have so much denial and rage that you do not know how to accept you, and so you stuff you and this creates certain problems for you. You are beginning to remove the programming that tells you how guilty and bad you are, and you will begin to replace guilty and bad with innocent and good. You will begin to reprogram you with information and insight. This information and insight comes from awareness of who you are and is not based on denying who you are.

You will find that as you create greater and greater awareness, you will literally be raising your own consciousness to an all-time high. You will begin to see how you are no longer being "put to the test" or "pushed at" by your own self. You will find that you begin to melt into your other half, and you begin to share your life instead of fighting for dominance over certain areas of your life. You will find that you can be one of the most unusual examples of "oneness." You will find that your oneness will come from the blending of all parts. Each individual part will begin to work together as a whole, and each individual part will pull its own weight.

Once you begin to "synchronize" all parts of you, you will begin to feel connected to the flow of creation. You will become part of all that is, and you will no longer be stuck and holding on to one particular place or thought or belief. You will be free to make choices and you will be free to go with the flow. Once you are flowing and allowing yourself to be moved along, you will see great improvement in your life. You will actually begin to feel as though you are being helped and guided. Listen to your guidance and know that you are loved by you as well as by your creator. You are loved and you do count. You are important and you are special. You have your part to play and your part makes a difference. You are not so much a one-man-show as you are a part-of-the-whole. You are one with God. Know this truth and you will find peace of mind and you will know heaven on earth.

When you begin to integrate and become whole, you will feel the difference. You will feel stronger, and you will feel more determined than ever to take care of all parts of you. You will begin to feel a sense of a life within a life. You will see how you are living in a world within yourself, as well as a world outside that is a projection from within. Once you begin to feel the difference, you will begin to know how to stay in creation, or, in creator. You will know how you play both positions, and you will begin to realize how you might take a conscious role in the creation of you. You are slipping into a position that will allow you to show yourself who and what you really are.

As you open up to face all parts of you, you actually get to face the God of you. You have always hidden God as you were hiding all the unwanted parts, and along with the unwanted parts go any part that is attached to them. If you created something you did not like, you may have shut off that part of you and, in the process, you may have closed down your abilities to create. You stifle you by shutting off things you cannot accept. Once you learn to accept all of creation, you will be accepting all of you. You cannot cancel out everything that upsets you and expect all the rest to not be affected. You are creating big changes in you by allowing you to be. You have parts of you that you cannot accept, but you can regain them by accepting them now and by understanding that judgment cuts you off from the rest of you and the rest of creation.

Once you begin to see how judgment works, you will be able to stop your judgment from creating for you. You see, all parts of you create. You even have parts that are suppressed, and yet they have the energy to create. You have parts who love and appreciate you as you love and appreciate them, and you have parts who hate you and want you gone as you hate them and want them gone. There is nothing else that is against you but you – no big enemy. You are your own enemy and you each carry this part of you. Paranoia and fear are you. You are afraid and upset because you carry this energy. This energy is what keeps you hostile and afraid to trust. Once you break through to the part of you that is paranoid, you will feel great mistrust. You will also be allowing your mistrust to leave simply by opening up to drain it.

My point here is to explain how, when you heal, you will "feel" what you are healing. If you are healing mistrust then mistrust is what you will predominantly feel. Allow your feelings to show you what you are healing. Do not shut down and push down what is trying to surface in order to heal. Allow all unhealed places to surface to the light of day. You have shut-down and turned-off so many parts of you, and they require time to heal and they require assistance in healing. You are not completely black and you are not completely white. You are both, so you will find your center somewhere between negative and positive. It will be a neutral position which is actually "no position."

Positionality will end when you come to center balance. You will no longer polarize, and you will no longer find it necessary to take a stand and fight. You will find that as you learn to flow, you will actually learn to love the flow, and you will learn to love you for flowing and you will learn to love life for flowing. Wouldn't you love to say, "Oh boy, my life is just flowing today?" You will find that you are no longer in the flow when you stop and dig-in, or take-a-stand on any given issue. Keep flowing. You are going places now, you are no longer stagnating.

*

I will begin to show you how you may become peace filled. You become peace filled by first emptying all parts of you that are at war or struggling to become known to you. Once this struggle to show yourself to yourself ends, you will begin to calm down and to allow more of you to come forward. Once you have exposed all parts of you to you, you will begin to relax because you will know that the enemy, you have always thought was out to get you, was only a part of you who was out to get your attention.

Once your attention is given to the order and placement of your parts, you will begin to feel a giant shift. As you experience this shift, you may begin to see how it is no longer necessary to fear any part of you that wishes to be exposed. This puts you in a position of great "relief" from "fear of exposure." Once you are no longer sitting in judgment of yourself, you will no longer find yourself guilty of anything. Once you proclaim your innocence (once you begin to let go of your belief that you are bad), you will no longer fear being exposed, for your shame will have left you – no more feelings of regret for your past and no more feelings of judging you for anything or everything you do. You will begin to set you free, and once you are free of guilt and shame, you will begin to know peace of mind and peace of spirit.

You have been taught to feel guilt and to feel remorse for what you do that is sinful. How can you not feel shame about being you if you are so strongly programmed to carry regret? If you do not carry regret, you feel like a villain or the big bad guy. You feel like the only way to be a good person is to repent and confess your sins. You even say that confession is good for the soul. Your only problem here is that no one explained that "you" forgive and forget. You forgive yourself, and you forget it and move on with your life. You are instead taught to remember and hold on to the feeling of wrong-doing, so that you will never do wrong again. You become a prisoner of your own convictions. You then suffer and "struggle" to get rid of the part of you who is reminding you what you did that felt (at the time) so bad.

There are parts of you who feel great guilt about something as small as punching out your little brother at age three, as well as other parts who feel just as guilty about the fact that you once cheated on your lover or spouse. You have gotten so good at carrying guilt that some of you carry guilt by association. This means that you actually feel and carry guilt that belongs to another's act. You only knew about a bad thing (or thought you knew) and you judged yourself as guilty because you did not tell anyone or confess to relieve the stress. Confession is good for your soul. I highly suggest that you confess to you all that *you* are holding against you. This will enable you to see how deep your judgment runs and to come out of denial. The more you know about your layers of shame and guilt, the greater your chance to let go of such pain. It is, after all, self-inflicted pain and it is very harmful to you.

When you begin to see how you are the one who is in charge of you, you will begin to change how you treat you. You are probably the one who is most critical of you, and you are probably the one who is most judgmental of your behavior. As you learn to know more about your own behavior towards your own self, you will begin to see how you could have forgotten patience and understanding in dealing with you. Now; once you become impatient and uncooperative within the self, you create a split. This split could be all the way across you or it could be a small fracture in your beingness. As far as I can observe, you are all split, and you have little to no tolerance with certain aspects of your own nature. Once you begin to heal this split you will begin to feel better about you.

You are no longer going to feel so upset or angry or guilty. You are going to begin to feel relief and lack of stress and tension. You are about to release the greatest tension causer in you. It is the ability to split and to push parts of you out of you. It is the ability to become what you are not in order to get what you seek. Some of you seek attention and some of you seek nurturing. You go to great lengths to receive the attention that brings adoration from one another. You are almost constantly seeking approval, and when you don't get it you are hurt. Once you receive approval you feel good! You feel appreciated.

Once you learn to approve of yourself and let go of judgment against parts of yourself, you will begin to heal this need to seek approval, or appreciation, elsewhere. You are only seeking the approval of another because you cannot consciously approve of your self. You are split. You disapprove of your self, and so your "self" is not in good standing with you, or the part of you who disapproves.

As you learn self-approval you will begin to heal this split, and you will no longer seek recognition in your field of expertise. You will begin to change how you react to certain gifts or talents. You will no longer have competitions. You will let go of your belief that those who excel in one area are better than others. You will develop characteristics within the spectrum, instead of taking parts out of the spectrum and showing them off to hold them at a higher level of appreciation.

You have been raised in an environment which praises those who achieve and denotes disdain for those who do not. This environment has been the breeding ground for discrimination, mistrust and separation. In your future you will create a new breeding ground. It will be in the middle – no great extremes of acceptable or unacceptable. You will be in the middle. It will not matter. You will be developing spiritual grace, and spiritual grace is centered in you and spiritual grace is centered in nature. Once you learn to be in spiritual grace, you will no longer feel the need to make one special and the other less than special. All human aspects will become not only acceptable; they will be considered a normal part of you. You will no longer call you bad for having a difficult trait. You will be much wiser in spirit, which will allow you to be a much better human being.

As you begin to separate parts of you, you actually begin to tear down your own essence. To separate you is to disown you or to split and fragment into sections of you. As you begin to reclaim all of your unwanted and pushed away parts, you actually begin to understand any part of life with a new fullness of meaning. Most of you are so fragmented that you lose yourself in just one meaning of any given situation.

Once you reintegrate and reclaim your parts, you will begin to see dual meaning in all of life. Your life is not only dual it is everything between any two opposites. You create from an entire line of energy not just one end of that energy. You will find that you do not always decipher your life from all possible variables. You usually determine one answer to any given question and then you hold to that answer no matter what. Things are about to change! You are about to gain access into a world of development and change. Flexibility is the keyword for success whenever you deal with change. Use your ability to flow with life and you will begin to know how to deal more adequately with life.

You are moving into a phase of your evolution which is extremely fragile, and if you wish to make it through without injury to your psyche, I highly suggest that you begin to get flexible. Flexibility will save you from your rigid side. You are stubborn and you are set in your ways and you are set in your beliefs. You must allow yourself to become "unset" which, for you, may feel like "unsettled." Do not fear. It is okay to not know all the answers, and it is okay to not always know what your next move will be. You are moving into the 21st century with a great deal of thrust. This will propel you well into your new spiritual position.

Once you begin to see how you are the one who is being changed, you will let go of your idea of how the universe will change. You create the universe from deep within you, and you project what is in you to the outside where the energy mixes with other energy and creates great things or small things. Energy is matter at its thinnest degree. Energy is matter in an ether form. When you work with energy you work with the base of all creation. You are energy and you create more energy. You are in it and you create it. You are what you create and you are the creator. You call it God and try to separate from it, but it is you. You are split. You pushed God out and thought you could split off into "him" and "us." It is not truth and it will not stand. You are him and he is you. You are split from God and you are healing your split. You are a fragment and now you will become whole.

※

Once you begin to integrate your male essence with your female essence, you will begin to see how you can actually live in the "center" of you. You will no longer feel like an extremist, and you will no longer be so out of balance that you are swinging from one extreme to the other. You will find that, as you come to the center of you, you will create from confidence and calmness. You will no longer require the zing that has driven you thus far. As you proceed from your center, you will find that you are not only being guided, you are also being taken care of by your own creative source. You will find that you no longer require excitement, and you will also find that you no longer required judgment to keep you "in-line" and "on track." You will automatically fall in line and be on track. You will be creating from your balanced essence of male and female. You will feel much more confident about who you are because you will be using much more of you than you ever dreamed possible.

Once you find your center, you will be off and running in a whole new dimension of your own self. You will find yourself very happy at times when you least expect it. You will begin to allow yourself to take in the gifts of life without judging them to death first. You will be on your way to becoming all that you can be. So far you have spent a great deal of time just being on one side of you. Now you get to come full circle and use the other side of you in connection with this side of you. You will be bringing all of you around to experience life instead of closing off parts of you.

You will find that as you grow into you more fully, you will actually be bringing forward more energy to use in your creation process. As this energy becomes more and more forceful, it actually begins to feel like you have power.

Do not misuse your power. You will know how to use it properly, as it is part of you and you are evolving into it. Do not be afraid to have power and do not lord it over another. You feel good when you get to feel smarter than, or richer than, or stronger than another. Do not confuse feeling good about being "on top" with being in a state of grace. When you are in a state of grace, you actually feel elevated and above fear. This is not the same as feeling elevated and above others. You are no longer using intimidation and other such techniques. You are getting far more honest, and you are using your sense of love and your sense of fairness.

    Once you begin to operate from love, you will automatically "play fair." You will no longer feel it necessary to pull the rug out from under another, nor to criticize and put down another just so you can feel better about yourself. Many of you do not realize that you do this, and if it were to be pointed out to you how often you put others down; you would go into denial to protect this game that you play. You, of course, put others down so you can feel "on top" or better about your self. The worse you feel about yourself, the greater will be your need to put others down. Once you begin to see how this works for everyone, you will be able to stop this form of manipulation. You are <u>constantly</u> manipulating and controlling to get your needs met. This could, in itself, be a book. It is so wound up in your daily habits and routines that you do not know you do half of what you do. You are a manipulator and you use this ploy often.

As you learn to spot yourself when you begin to do this sport of manipulation, you will begin to see how frequent it goes on. You are moving into a part of you who is more balanced and, therefore, manipulation and control must find their proper place. Their place is not in your personal relationships as you believe. Their place is in you, to allow you to transform certain events in your life into positive growth experiences. You will not find manipulation used on others in the future. It was meant to guide you to a part of you that could change how "you" saw things, not how others saw things. Once you bring manipulation and control back to you, and stop using them on others, you will find that they will actually come to rest in you and they will no longer be as big as they now are.

You are moving into love, and love will absorb whatever parts it can. The more love you uncover, the greater its ability to take over.

※

When you begin to see how you are no longer in a place where you must constantly protect and defend yourself, you will allow yourself outside your wall of protection. Your wall was meant to keep you safe and to keep others away from you. This is how you take care of your self when you are afraid of hurt or pain. If you are heavily programmed to be in your protection mode, you will find it difficult to let down your guard and to be unsafe, or vulnerable, in any given situation.

Once you manage to reprogram yourself, you will be showing your self how protection is no longer your number one goal, and you will also be putting you in a much calmer place. You need not ever be protected in the way you now are. Walls of protection become prison walls, and you become lonely behind them. Once you have learned how to become free of your protection ploys, you will begin to feel much freer and actually safer. You are so bent on feeling safe in your emotional body that you no longer feel your emotional body. You convince yourself that you feel this way or that way when, in actuality, you are completely off base with your assessment of your feelings. You are mostly disguising what you feel, so you do not have to admit that you are the one who is hurting you, by the sheer pressure you put on you to keep you in line and following your rules.

Once you begin to see how you are no longer in need of self-punishment, you will begin to give you a rest. Your self-punishment only comes out of a need to relieve your guilt. Your guilt leaves when you begin to realize that you are innocent. Once you have forgiven your self, you will automatically become safe from self-inflicted punishment.

As this process of self-forgiveness continues, you will begin to see remarkable changes in who you are and how you behave. As you set greater freedom standards for yourself you will be allowed to actively allow yourself freedom, and you will also be allowed to show yourself some of what you have been missing all your life. As you continue to be enlightened and relieved of your old rules, you will begin to see how you are only being foolish to keep such rules. Many of you believe you must interrelate with restriction on your behavior so you will not appear foolish, when, in actuality, the fool is the one who is afraid to make a foolish move. Often a foolish move turns out to be a blessing in disguise.

As you begin to discover your misguided sense of over-protectiveness, you will see how you are actually very foolish when it comes to how you protect you from your feelings. Some of you never experience emotional pleasure simply because you will not trust another with your feelings. The problem is not 'trusting another with your feelings,' it is instead what you do with your own feelings. You are the one who has the power to turn any given situation into one of pleasure, or pain, simply by how you feel. How you feel is not often the truth, because you lie to yourself about how you feel in order to protect yourself from knowing the truth.

The truth is that you are innocent and you have never, ever done anything wrong. The truth is that you are stuck in a play and cannot get out of your role as victim, or perpetrator. The truth is that you are now learning to evolve out of such games of fooling your self. The truth is that you are right when you begin to allow yourself to be wrong. The truth is that you are stuck and you want out. So often you kill yourselves to get out. You want out of your feelings. You do not want to own feelings, so you shut them off and say, "I don't feel, therefore, you cannot hurt me."

The truth is that he or she can never hurt your feelings. You choose how you want to feel according to what you need (this need is usually unconscious) and then you zap you with a dose of self-pity, or self-defiance, or whatever will get you up and over your current set of uncomfortable feelings. You then begin to judge your feelings and create reassurance, in your physical form, that you will never again allow these upsetting feelings. You are then duly programmed to ignore, or refrain from, anything that may stir these feelings. This way you do not have to feel them again.

This is part of your protection. Then, if the situation in a relationship arises in which you are stimulated to feel any of these plugged-up and shut-down feelings, you begin to push those feelings further down by making them bad or wrong or stupid. That way you can more easily turn them off, or into something that is not good for you. This keeps you safe and free of these unwanted feelings for now; but they are still in you and you will have to keep up your drug intake of alcohol and cigarettes and pills if you want to continue to suppress them, or yourself, so you will not feel.

So why do you do drugs and stimulants? It is simply a way of hiding what you feel from you. The greater your need for your addictions, the greater your need to stay separate and shut-off and closed-down from parts of you. Stop trying to shut down your feelings. It is killing you and turning you into programmed robots. You are no longer in touch with you. You have shut down "feeling" and made it into something bad. Come back to feeling. Allow yourself to feel, and give up this unrealistic need to protect yourself from your self. You are "one" if you will only allow yourself to be all parts of you.

When you learn to see how you act-out, you will begin to know where your weak points are. Once you realize that not all that is considered foolish or soft is actually weakness, you will begin to see how you can be humble and not be a weak person. You were all taught to be tough and not show fear or weakness, men more so than women. But it is still the same programming that invades you all. It tells you to act strong or you will be pushed around and made to be a victim. In actuality, you are only as weak as you are strong. Your weakness and your strength are the same line of energy. If you have built up your strength in one area, or end of your life, you have more than likely weakened in another area. You will find that you no longer know how to deal with life, in certain realms, if your strength is severely focused in one area.

As you learn to be more balanced and bring your energy back to center, you will begin to see how you are not only 'not' too stable right now, you are also very unstable. Your energy is all pushed in one direction and it is now pulling you off in that direction. It is as if you carried big bags of heavy energy on your shoulders, and one side is heavier and you are gradually tilting to that side. You begin to tilt too far, and the heavy bag of energy will pull you down as it falls to one side. Now you are one-sided, and you are unable to see how you got so far down on this side of you.

You will want to release old ways in order to release your hold on the weight that has pulled you down all along. Once you can lighten the off-balance load, you can bring it to center and begin to work from balance. As you take off old ways and begin to lighten up, you will actually feel quite good about yourself. You will literally feel lighter and softer. The heavy load makes you feel tough and hard, but that is part of this illusion of strength. The softer you get, the more pliable you are. The more pliable you become, the greater your possibility of instantaneous healing and rising up. Pliability is a very good thing and it allows you to be soft and gentle. You no longer require a harsh attitude or harsh words. You are soft and you feel soft feelings. Your pointed, sharp ways relax and become soft ways. You actually are perceived as having strength of character when you don't flip-out at every turn. Softness will do this for you.

As you learn to unload your bags of energy in order to balance, you will want to be gentle with and not critical of yourself. You will want to allow yourself to "shift" into a less tough role. You will also want to allow yourself to be "the fool." This is due to the fact that you all have soft things that make you feel foolish, and you are so programmed to not allow yourself to be the "foolish one." Give it a try. Break down. Be a little foolish and soften up a lot! You need it.

---

*W*hen you lose your desire to control and dominate, you will begin to see how you have always been loving and kind. Your desire to dominate makes you feel superior and allows you to rise above low self-esteem. If you have someone you can easily manipulate and control, you feel powerful. This someone may be a child, a pet, a lover, a friend or even a parent. You are all programmed in this way because you grew up being manipulated and controlled. You were expected to learn and to grow into a fine citizen, and often whatever it took to get you to cooperate is what was done.

Children have a way of doing what they want and when they want. You, of course, want order and a respectable child, so you reprimand and use whatever techniques you have learned to train them to be responsible. Your parents did this and now you do this. Some of you hate how you were raised, and so you seem to be more lenient and less strict, but are you really, or do you simply act-out the strictness (you were programmed with) in other areas that were not important to your parents?

When you begin to see how you manipulate and control to get things your way, you may want to ask, "Is this really what I want and why do I think I want it?" You may be manipulating and controlling for the sheer pleasure of feeling in charge. Look at the greater picture and see how you really feel about the situation or the person you are working wiles on. Do you do this to gain control or do you do this to feel good about who you are? Do you want what you are after, or do you want to win; to be in charge; to get your own way? Who are you manipulating and controlling? Is it you or is it them?

Sometimes, in your attempt to get what you want, you begin to act differently and be what you think another might want you to be. Are you giving in to pressure (from your own self) to be what you do not want to be in order to get what you want? How does it feel? Does it feel good and relief like, or does it feel bad and tense like? If it feels good to be different, or act different, you will want to let it be. If it feels tense and restrictive, you will want to back out and re-evaluate whether or not you really want it. Be "it" a situation in a relationship, a situation at work, or a situation in you personally, you no longer have to force you into pigeonholes and cause you to be a carbon copy of anyone else. Learn to be who and what you are. Do not be afraid to be you, and do not be afraid to love you enough to be you.

I will now tell you how you will begin to rise above evil. You will rise above what you call evil by not buying into it. If you do not believe in the evil side of anything, you do not create evil. You do not create the fear that goes with the creation of evil, and you do not create the mistrust that follows. If you can learn to see everyone and everything as created energy, you will begin to let go of your belief in evil. Learn to see that everyone and everything is responding to life force and to everything else in the universe. Everything touches everything. Nothing is left out. So if you judge part of creation as bad, or evil, it is then part of you because you touch everything. Once you can learn to let go of your need to put yourself down and make yourself wrong or bad, you will let go of your need to make others wrong or bad. You are trying to fix you, and you project this need for fixing out onto others. Once you get that, you will focus on you and the rest will take care of itself.

As you learn how to let go of your need to punish you, you automatically let go of your need to punish another. Once you have found a place in which you feel good about yourself, you will automatically begin to feel good about another. Once you have forgiven you, you will automatically forgive them. You are them and they are you. Once you find your place to be yourself, without judgment against yourself, you will actually be accepting yourself. And what is self-acceptance? Yes, it is love.

So; as you let go of evil and your letting go of evil renews your trust, you will automatically slip into acceptance of the self. Once you are accepting you, you will be able, or free, to accept all that comes your way. You will no longer struggle with yourself about what is right or wrong for you. It will now become a decision of whether or not you want it. It will not be based on fear of getting or not getting. It will now be based on simple acceptance if it is what you like.

It will feel so easy in the beginning that you may slip back into your old pattern of wondering if you made a mistake in your choice. You will also fear failure in your new choices, but, in the long run, you will begin to see the pattern of acceptance, and this simple trust and faith acceptance will allow you to create more of the same. So now, instead of mistrust, we have you creating trust and faith. Once you have trust and faith you will have the tools you require to build a bright and love-filled future. You are on the edge of your future now and it looks very, very good!

When you first begin to touch parts of you that have been unavailable to you until now, you will begin to feel very uncomfortable. These parts have not been seen by you for a very long time, and they are considered shut-off.

Once they turn-on, you will feel as though you are not in control. You shut them off to keep you safe and to keep you free of pain. Now these parts are moving again and they may carry pain. Once you begin to move them, you may want to remove them from your life. You will do best to allow them to express their pain and to allow them to be what they were meant to be. They are meant to be a functioning part of you, and they got pushed out of you, or so deep into you that they believe they are out of you.

Once you begin to work with these parts, you will automatically begin to take the charge off of them. Once you begin to receive them as a part of you, you will be telling them that they do belong and they are not separate from the rest of you. Once you own these parts, you will be owning you and healing you in the process of accepting them. You will begin to accept more of you and this will allow you to love more of you. As you grow in love, you will automatically be putting yourself in a position of healing. Love is how you heal, and love is how you begin to accept the unacceptable.

Once you learn to be more accepting, you will see how your world will open up to you. You have closed down and shut off, and now you are opening up and turning on. It feels strange to you. You have never been full of yourself. You have never allowed you in. You have fragmented, and split, and separated parts for so long that you no longer know how to get all of you to return to you. It is as though you sent out scouts and they never returned to tell you what to watch for ahead. They simply disappeared. They never returned to give you correct answers because they thought you did not want them in you. So they hid in places deep in you so they would not be discovered. They try very hard to stay still and not move, so that you will not send them away again. Now you are regaining these parts by allowing them to stay. Once you learn how to work with them, you will no longer wish to push them away. Once you learn to accept them, you will find them an added gift in your life.

This is how you heal. You look at and touch the unhealed places, and the touching allows them to know they are not dead. They are alive and they begin to move again and to take part in your life again. These parts are life force that you are turning back "on." You have turned off, and shut off, so many parts of you that it is good to begin to re-ignite these parts and turn them back on. You are becoming whole and this means accepting all parts of you, even those you believe should not exist. If you did not judge you, and slowly shut off parts, you would be whole and complete. Now you are learning to allow you to be whole and complete. You are missing part of you and you seek to find this part in others. Do not be afraid to love all of you and you will find that all of you will return, and you will no longer seek outside of yourself.

*O*nce you begin to discover your true essence, you will no longer worry about doing the right thing or the wrong thing. You will do what brings joy and you will do what brings love. As you learn to let go of your fear of life, you will see yourself begin to unravel most of what has caused you to be afraid. You will also see yourself begin to know how you respond to any given situation. Once you see how you respond, you can begin to focus on ways to change so you will no longer be acting-out. Most often you are responding by allowing your buttons to be pushed.

Once you are discharged in certain areas, it will no longer matter whether or not you get your buttons pushed. You will be disarmed and unable to fight or blow-up. You will not be a victim or an unwilling participant. You will simply no longer feel the pressure to blow. Once you are totally discharged you will feel very good indeed. You will be released of anything that makes you blow-up or compress in. You will actually feel so good about yourself that you no longer have a place in you that feels bad about you. The only time you explode, or get upset, is when someone or something mirrors back how bad you feel about you.

Once you learn to be who you are and to love who you are, you will no longer be upset by anything anyone says or does. You will finally be in control of you, and this control will not be so exhausting as trying to make you behave in a specific way. This control will be more like a guidance that gives you, or shows you, the way. This control is more like driving your car down a road where you thoroughly enjoy the scenery and the drive itself. It will no longer be work to keep you in between the lines. You will easily and gracefully stay in your lane, and no longer will you run others off the road, or jam up traffic by your attitude about driving. You will, for once, be living in a world of ease and grace. You will be riding the joy ride, and you will not get into an accident and there will be no flat tires. You will find yourself in a position of flowing with all life and you will love it. This will, of course, be after you are defused and ready to see your true essence.

You will find that as you begin to defuse various parts of you, you will literally bring situations to you so you may *see* how and what pushes your buttons. The greater number of times you can get your buttons pushed and bring up the explosive feelings, the greater the release on the emotional charge that is in place.

So; no matter how much you hate these feelings, you are actually doing yourself a great service by experiencing them. Go ahead and feel your bad feelings. They are not really bad you know? You just call them bad because you are afraid of them. Watch how you are set off, and watch to see how you respond once you are set off. You will find that you are programmed. If you were raised around someone who was strong in a particular way of seeing life, the chances are great that you took on the beliefs of that individual. If you had strong role models you are probably carrying their fears and their beliefs. If you had a father who refused to be made to look foolish, you may literally "hurt" when you think someone is talking behind your back, or making fun of you in any way. You are programmed to believe what you believe, and you are programmed to think the way that you think.

Once you find your essence, or your true self, you will be able to quickly heal you by allowing your true self to take over and to assist in healing the false self. This is done through a process of elimination. Once you begin to connect with the true self, you will find that you will be free to bring up more and more of the false self. As you bring up more and more of the false self, you will be able to heal that which is false. You set this in motion by wanting to heal and by wanting to love.

Once you begin this process, you will find it easier and easier as you go along. You bring up the false, or the lie, and it dissolves into the light of truth. You will find that as you develop a connection with the truth, you will no longer be afraid of the lies. Lies will not hurt you once you let go of your fear of being hurt. You are in the process of releasing pain from your body now. Do not fear that this pain is you. It is the false belief. It is in place to stop you from doing or saying certain things. This pain must leave, and in order to leave it must be re-experienced. How do you feel about feeling your pain in order to let it go?

How would you like to be free of hurt feelings and hard feelings? How would you like to feel good about yourself no matter how your life is going? How would you like to never be upset? Do you think it is impossible? It is not. You will learn to walk in peace and love, and you will let go of hard feelings, and you will begin to love you even more than you now think you do. You will begin to feel free of your old beliefs and this will allow you to become happy. Freedom is synonymous with happiness. Once you become free you will feel as though you can do anything. Once you become free you will be looking at you in a whole new light.

As you seek freedom, you may begin to see some of the chains of restriction you have used on yourself. Once you begin to let go of your restrictions, you will find yourself quite well received by others and by your own self. As you learn to set you free of this type of restraint, you will begin to see new ways to deal with yourself and new ways to be unafraid of yourself and your own natural ways. As you learn to set you free, you will be setting all parts of you free. You will be learning that it is safe to allow certain parts of you to be unrestrained and set free.

As you begin to unwind this big mass of entangled beliefs that tells you how you must act and what you must do, you will begin to see how you are working with yourself instead of against yourself as you have always done in the past. As you allow yourself to be free and to express your feelings, you will begin to see how you are actually setting your true essence free. Whenever you tie up any part of you it is connected to other parts, and they all become restrained and held back from doing their job. What if you were sexually abused, or emotionally abused, and you (as a child) believed it was your fault? You would then grow up believing it is all your fault, so you have to watch how you behave because you are the cause of problems for yourself. You will stifle emotions and play games because you do not know how to simply be yourself. This in itself creates problems for you. You begin to see how others operate and you watch and learn to copy. Who do you copy? Well, if you are very young you copy the gods of your world. Your primary caregivers are your gods.

So; if you had a manipulative parent or caregiver, you can bet that you are now manipulative. Maybe you manipulate differently, but you still do it. You probably manipulate your own emotions a great deal to convince them to leave you alone. Emotionally and sexually abused children grow up to abuse what they were taught to abuse. If it was sex, they abuse sex by turning it into something awful or by misusing it. If they were emotionally abused they will mistreat the emotions. You may find that both are at work, especially in incest and sexual abuse, since emotions play a big part in your relationships to others.

So now you grow up and you have this place in you that is all confused and full of pain. You hide it as much as you can because it makes you feel awful about yourself. You even try to make yourself look more attractive, so no one will notice this ugly place in you that is all knotted up and mangled. Once you begin to unknot this place you will feel better. It is emotionally tied up in a knot. Your body may respond by becoming tense and knotted while you work on undoing this knot that has been in you all your life. As you gradually untangle your knot, you will feel its tension in you as it begins to unravel. Stay calm and do not overreact. Just be calm and stay as relaxed as you can. Do a meditation or put yourself in a warm tub of salt water to detox and unwind.

You will find that the emotional body is highly charged and it likes to feel itself to know it is still here. It will often create situations to allow it to feel itself. It will often create situations of over reaction just to get a good feel for where you are emotionally. Do not be afraid to move your emotional body, and be aware that you are clearing away a big mess and may try to draw an emotional situation to you in the process. This will all be explained as we go. For now, I wish you a good day and good luck as you begin to unknot you!

☙❧

Once you begin to see how you are no longer tied to your old knotted up programming, you will begin to unwind and relax. Most of your tension is due to unresolved issues within you that are keeping you from flowing with life. Once you learn how to be free of your unresolved issues you will no longer feel tension. These issues are primarily attached to a belief, and this belief usually says that you are at fault for something. Once you allow the knotted up part to relax, it will be easier to unwound, or undo, the knot. It is not so unusual to have several knotted up areas in you. These are areas of tension, and they are most commonly seen in tense or uncomfortable situations. Actually, they are the part of you that make the situations *appear* tense or uncomfortable.

Once you learn how to relax your pull on this particular line of energy, you will be allowing the entire knotted area to rest and to breathe. This is done by not forcing yourself to behave in a specific way. Usually this has to do with any programming that makes you feel safe, or right, or untouchable. As you back out of any situation, you usually begin to feel relief. Once you learn how you create the tension, you will no longer feel such a strong need to leave or back out. Once you discover how energy works and how it creates for you, you will see the benefit in letting go of the fear rather than letting go of the entire situation. Many of you just cannot handle certain situations simply out of fear of not performing well. You will find that your performance is no longer being judged, and you are no longer being punished by you for being you. This will make everything inside of you much easier. It will also make it much easier for you to be you.

As you begin to forgive you for all that you deem as bad, you will be giving you a much needed break from criticism and lack of self-approval. Once you begin to approve of yourself, it will become apparent and it will be noted by others as well as by yourself. You will begin to feel better once the knots of energy begin to relax and slowly unwind. It will be a big relief, but it will also feel draining. You will lose a very tense ball of energy, so you may feel as though you are exhausted or drained. Fear energy pushes you forward in the same way that you are motivated to move by pain. It will take you awhile to replace the fear (created by judgment) with love.

Once you have let go of this build-up of energy, you will be able to replace it with lighter energy, and you will be able to work *with* this lighter energy instead of it opposing you. This will all take place as the built-up pressure points begin to subside. Once you let go of your need to pull or push at you to do better, or achieve greater acclamation for your deeds, you will be letting the pressure off or relaxing your pull at you. Once you relax the pull, or push, you will feel better, and then you will begin to relax enough to feel your love and your own approval. Right now you are so pulled in one direction that you cannot possibly approve of you. This will all change and you will come back to balance. Then you will be in a position to receive from the main flow of creation. This will become a very good time for you, and you will begin to heal the split within you that has caused you to mistrust and abuse your own self.

When you begin to feel how your defenses are coming down, you may actually feel more vulnerable than usual. You may feel as though you are more sensitive than usual, and you may feel that you do not really know your own self. You may actually feel very confused and very upset with yourself. As you learn to let go of your need to protect yourself, you will see that this need for protection is based on false beliefs and false ideas. Now you are in a position to release what is not necessary and to heal your pain. Once you begin to put down your protection, you are much more likely to draw love to you. Your protection will keep you safe and it will keep you in a place where you will find only fear. When you find it necessary to protect yourself, you are also finding it necessary to be away from love. Love requires only pureness and love does not require protection.

Once you create protection, you begin to block the flow of energy through you. This eventually has a chain reaction effect on all energy within you. You begin to form blocks to compensate for energy shortages, and you begin to take on excessive roles to allow shifts in energy. As you push all of your energy to one side of you, in order to block or protect, this energy then begins to require release. Often you become possessive and withholding in areas where energy is blocked. You go to extremes by the mere fact that the energy is all pushed to one side of you. You may become obsessive in behavior and compulsive as well. You don't actually consider yourself to be out of balance because you think you are doing the good and right thing by protecting you and shutting down what you cannot handle.

After years of being one-sided, you begin to see how your life is one-sided and you have parts missing. You know you could do better in life if you could just have this or that at your disposal, and what you actually need is to let go of your need to protect you. This requires trust! You must learn to trust that God is with you and in you. You must learn to let go of your need to separate you further. You must now begin to accept all parts of you. You will know when you are accepting all of you, because you will be accepting all that is part of living as well as dying.

Once you accept you, you will begin to see tremendous changes in you. You will feel lovable and acceptable which will allow you to feel good about yourself. No matter how self-conscious you now feel in certain situations, you will begin to see how this is simply a reflection of your lack of self-esteem. Once you hold yourself in high regard, you will not feel less than worthy of any given gift. You would be able to freely accept a new car from a total stranger if you held yourself in high esteem. You would be able to accept gold, or even a new home from someone you hate if you held yourself in high esteem. Actually, you would find it difficult to hate anyone if you found yourself held in high esteem.

Once you learn to change how you view you, you will be on the path to changing how you view all life. It all begins in you with your belief in good or bad. Let everything be good and you will be giving you a good life. You want the good life... it's yours for the taking. Let go of the bad that you hold on to. It makes you require energy shifts in the body that put you off-balance, and you do not operate from love when you are not in your center.

As we grow we begin to see how we are not exactly full-grown (even though you may be fifty or sixty or even seventy years of age) you will learn that you do not mature as you thought. You actually continue to grow and evolve and rise up in a spiritual manner. Your physical being may consider itself finished, but once it plugs into the spiritual realms, it then begins to live all over again. It must then re-grow certain aspects and parts to fit into the new paradigm. Once you have used your own spiritual juice to get you started in the re-growth process, you will begin to change (gradually) in every area of your life.

Once you plug into the spiritual aspects of your own life, you will begin to change and grow in areas you did not know existed. You will become whole by reconnecting with your spirit. You will become whole by knowing how you are God and by allowing yourself to be continually changed. You are in such a fragmented state that change will hurt until you become more connected to the rest of you. The more you reconnect, the easier it becomes to flow with life and with change. You also learn to not attach to what you create. You no longer project into your creation and make it everything, or all important. You begin to mellow and to harmonize with life. You will find balance, and you will come out of your state of unconscious behavior and programmed needs. You will begin to see how you fit into creation, and you will allow yourself to take on the role of spirit, without having fear regarding this role.

Once you learn to be free of fear, you will be allowed to experience all that will make you whole. Most of you are afraid to feel God in you, and you are most certainly afraid to feel God's presence outside of you. If you connect too strongly with spirit, you will upset your own condition. Your present condition is one of controlled anxiety and controlled circumstance. You only allow circumstances to occur which you can handle to some degree, and which are good feeling. So, often, it takes spirit a long time to connect with you and to take charge in your life. You will only go so far in your fear of pain and hurt. To dissolve your fear of pain and hurt, you must learn to face your pain and hurt. This is a very big problem area for you.

Once you can learn to see how you avoid pain and hurt, you will see how you are actually avoiding areas of living. This line of energy runs both ways, and there are those of you who now use pain and hurt to get attention and to gain in your life. Some use pain and hurt to make others feel responsible, and others use pain and hurt to make themselves feel better. You can punish yourself and never know that you are. You can justify your use of energy and habits and patterns to the extent that you literally withhold your own good, and you will not know that it is all you who is creating your victim role.

As you begin to come into this dawning of the New Age, I hope you remember that you are just coming into you. You are just being born of spirit. I don't care if you are twelve or one hundred and twelve, you are "becoming" and you are growing and changing. As you continue to move and change and grow, you will be fulfilling your own prophecy. You will be coming into creation. You are God consciousness entering God manifestation. You are God inseminating itself into creation. You are God being born in you and you are God growing in you. Your life will become a life of ease and your spirit will be fulfilled. You will rise up in consciousness by the mere fact that you are taking on consciousness. You are taking on the mind of God and all that is God. You are receiving spirit, and this requires expansion of intelligence and wisdom. This is a time of growth for you. When you grow you change. Do not be afraid to change. Do not be afraid to let your guard down. Do not be afraid to face your fears.

When you begin to do your final integration, you will begin to see how you have never before been so "together." You have always been fragmented and not together. This coming together will lift you to new levels of understanding, and you will begin to see the use of intelligence in the production of creation.

Once you have begun to integrate, you will more readily and more easily know who you are and how you are behaving. You will no longer respond from old programming, as your information will now be more complete. The more of you that you take on, the greater your base of information. Once you learn to recognize your own use of intelligence in creating your reality, you will no longer wish to mix your intelligence with ignorance. Most of what you have created in the past has had big gaps of non-information in it. It has come from misinformation and unconscious behavior. You will find that as you create from intelligence, you will get a full version of what you are creating, instead of a fragment of what you want. When you are fragmented you create fragmented realities, and when you are whole you create whole realities.

Once you learn to understand the difference between love and desire, you will begin to create from love and let go of your need to create from desire. As you move into your wholeness, you will feel love replace desire. You will feel as though you are moving into a whole new dimension within your own life. You will feel as though you are beginning to come full circle in your need for receiving and giving love. Once you feel yourself begin to move into love, you will automatically feel kindness fill you. You will have within you so much to share and so much to give that you will begin to take care of yourself in very loving ways. You will find it easy to be kind to yourself, and you will no longer be afraid to love yourself first. You will begin to know the joy of self-love, and you will begin to know the joy of self-acceptance.

Once you feel yourself moving into love and out of desire, you will be headed home. Your long struggle with you will be over, and you will find yourself at ease and in harmony. You will begin to know your own sense of identity, and you will no longer struggle to understand why you do what you do, and you will not struggle to understand why others do what they do. You will be in a state of acceptance, and you will know you for the first time since you were born. Most of you do not accept yourselves now, but when you do, you will begin to feel your power.

As far back as you can go, you have always played some kind of "poor me" or "victim" role. Now you are discovering that you create your reality and you are your own worst enemy. So now you find that you are able to create something, or even un-create something, simply by your attitude and forethought. Once you learn to change your thoughts, you will be changing what you project forward. Thoughts and ideas are not conscious in you. You have greater amounts of disharmony, and mistrust, coming from the unconscious ideas you have buried. They are unconscious because you have knocked them out of you (conscious you) in order to silence them. They are very much a part of you and they are very real. They project images which you face and deal with on a daily basis.

As you learn to accept your unconscious self, you will begin to see how it has run your life. You have always allowed it to control a great deal without your awareness that it does. Now it is time to wake up and know that you are a walking, talking time bomb, and you are ready to blow at the least provocation. You, of course, will blame this on your neighbor, or situations that trigger you, but you will soon learn that it is all your own anger at your own self that sets you off. Once you have defused the situation in *you*, by allowing yourself to release old pent-up parts of yourself, you will begin to see how you can actually begin to change how you create and what you create. You can begin to create love, and let go of your great need for fear to keep you in line and moral. You will let go of your need for a condemning God and a judging God. You will change God's role to love and let go of everything else. You will begin to see through the eyes of love and you will let go of all else.

As you learn to integrate the various parts of your nature and to accept them, you will begin to see only love and acceptance. You will come into a place in your nature that allows for the wholeness of everything. The wholeness says guilt and innocence are the same thing. You may take this line of energy and say someone is innocent, or you may take it to show how guilt prevails. Either way you are going from one polarity to another.

Guilt "is" and innocence "is." Do not make more of anything than what it is. Let it go and let it "be." Let everything simply "be" and you will no longer get stuck in one side or the other. You will no longer be pushed off-balance, and you will learn how to stay in the middle. You will find that you are happiest when you are centered and balanced. As the saying goes, "Do you want to be right or do you want to be happy?" Nothing is a matter of guilt or innocence. Everything "is." You do not determine creation by wrong or right, or you will kill off half of creation. Guilt is a state of belief. Innocence is a state of belief. You do not subject creation to your rules and then call it "for God," or "morally right." It does not balance.

You must learn to let go of judgment in order to find your center and work from wholeness. Do not separate and judge or you will be going deeper into fear. We are coming out of fear, and it is best to no longer find guilt or innocence. This confuses you, but it will all make sense when you are centered and whole. From the position of centeredness, you can see where all roads lead and you can see where the detours and roadblocks are. You can also see where wrecks and stalls will occur; this is how you learn to stay where you can see. Once you go off half-cocked in the direction you believe in, you begin to become one-sided and blind to what is going on. Stay in the center. In the center there is no wrong or right. In the center there is no bad or good. In the center there is no innocence or guilt. In the center there is no judgment. In the center there is peace because there are no polarities. In the center there is love and love is all there is.

When you become acquainted with all parts of you, you will no longer feel so unsure about who you are. Your uncertainties are part of your frailties. Once you learn that you are all part of one big mechanism and you are no longer fighting for control, you will begin to mellow out and relax into your life. You will still feel it necessary to stir things up once in awhile, but it will no longer be your primary goal. You will begin to see how you are the one who creates all of your disturbances, and you are the one who creates your calm and peace. Sometimes your calm and peace is most difficult for you. You get bored and want excitement and zing! Now you are learning to let go of your requirement for zing in your life, and you may not be happy without the excitement you have always held on to. You may long for more in your life once you begin to let go of struggle.

When you have struggle within, you have extreme fatigue and up-lift at the same time. Once you let go of your need-to-keep-going-in-order-to-keep-your-defenses-up, you may find that you feel like you have no purpose. This is part of letting go. There is always a let down and sorrow after you have let go of something big. Even if the thing you are letting go of was hurting you all along. You are attached and you will miss it. If you were verbally beating you up to keep you in line, you will miss it when you let go of this pattern. If you were physically beating you up to keep you in line, you will miss that part of you also. You will miss what you have always known, for that is the part of you who has always been engaged with you in some way. It's like losing your neighbors who have always been there through your ups and your downs.

When you finally learn to allow peace in your mind, you will find it vacant and not too stimulating. You are accustomed to a great deal of action within you, and to slow down that action feels like you are giving up. You have always fought for control of you and to be the best you think you should be. Once you begin to give up this struggle, you will feel like you are becoming the nothing you were always afraid you might become.

When you have a need to be special it is very difficult for you to settle for less than special, especially if you now think you are becoming less than what is ordinary. You always wanted to be special, and now you are slipping to below ordinary and it will not feel good for you. It will, however, be very good for you to let go of these patterns and behaviors that cause your struggle within. Once you learn to allow them to go, you will feel the let down and then the sorrow of loss. Once loss has been accepted, you will begin to fill this area in you with balance and light. You will find that it is a very big part of you, and it will take time to heal and refill it. It will also take time for your physical body to adjust to the loss of such big programming. After all, it's like losing a kidney or other vital organ for your body. This big part was always there and it took energy and distributed energy, and now it is gone.

You must allow your body time to heal. If you are one who has always hurt yourself physically in order to keep you in line, you will feel exhausted after you lose this part that has beaten you up. You have literally allowed this part to be in charge and to hold you up at times. Sure, this part of you punished you and hurt you, but it also gave you strength by allowing you to defend yourself on a constant and ongoing basis. Once it is gone you will need to refill this part, or place in you, with something that will give you strength. Peace will give you strength and peace will bring balance. Peace will feel boring after the constant struggle and friction. Try to "give peace a chance." Try to accept peace and not push it out in order to receive friction and stimulus. Give peace a chance to begin to feel good to you. You will like peace once you have spent time in peace. Do not be so quick to judge peace. It is not boring to be in peace. It is actually very peaceful and can be very uplifting.

***

As I begin to become part of you and part of your daily life, I will be in you and of you. I will make my will known in various ways, and I will begin to heal all parts of you. I do not concentrate on just one or two parts, and I do not assert my wishes on you without your consent. I work with you; I do not work against you. You will find that as I become a part of you, you will actually begin to feel my presence. I will be quiet and I will not bully you. I will, however, be up to my old tricks of making you happy and making you love. I will not try to force happiness or love on you, and I will not try to force myself on you. You are part of me and I am part of you. You are love and I am love. You are going to become more of your own essence and less fear. The more love you take on, the less fear you will hold. This is an automatic situation.

Once you have overcome your requirement for splitting off parts, you will begin to appreciate God. It is difficult at this time to appreciate what you believe to be feared. You are taught such reverence toward a vengeful monster who throws you in hell, or finds your misdeeds, that it is very difficult for you to drop your need to fear me and to simply accept me as a part of you. So; as you begin to integrate with God, I do suggest that you allow for change. Your fears will come up as God enters. Be brave and allow your fears to express. You need not like or embrace your fears, but do try to allow them to speak. Allow your fear to be known to you and do not suppress it down in you. You will be digging up a great deal of fear when you begin to integrate with God.

God is not so much a big part of you now as he will be in your future. God is being born into you a little at a time. Once you begin to feel how you are changing and becoming softer, you will know that God is in and has a good foothold inside of you. Once God has arrived in you, your split within the self will automatically begin to heal. God will allow pain to rise up and leave while making space for joy to enter. Pain does not always feel itself, and pain does not always know that it is pain. Often you will find parts of you that are unaware that they hold pain.

As the pain from these parts surfaces, it may take you by surprise. You may have expected joy and received pain at some point in childhood, and so your signals are now confused. Do not be afraid to see the truth and do not be afraid to know yourself. To know you is to love you, and to love you is to accept you. In the acceptance of you, you will learn to heal and to expand. As you expand, you automatically take on more of you or your essence. You have dropped off so many parts of you that you are fragmented and quite small. If you re-collect (recollect) major parts of you, who split during childhood, you can actually begin to feel very young again. You can go into a phase of development that requires growth of this newly recollected or recalled part.

As you heal this part, you grow with it and it grows within you. You actually become your own parent to this newly retrieved part, and you may teach it all that you now know so it will not be so full of your old programming. Some parts are very big and have stayed far away, while others are small and have been nudging at you all your life. They will do whatever is necessary to get your attention in order to return. When you lose a big part, it is usually due to a big trauma. If you were severely reprimanded or threatened as a child, you may have a big chunk of you missing. If you were sexually abused, or manipulated in an offensive way, you probably have several big chunks of you missing. If you were bullied and threatened, to the extent that you lived in fear, you definitely have big chunks missing.

As these big parts of you begin to return, you will begin to feel them as young, hopeful or even silly. You begin to think immaturely and to be immature in your reactions. This is due to the return of a part who left in childhood. This part did not get to grow with you and mature. When you retrieve this part, you will find yourself (part of yourself) acting very immature. Do not judge you for acting immature, enjoy this returned part, as it will grow and integrate into you quite quickly. You are becoming more of you, and the more you become the closer to wholeness you will be. This is a time for wholeness, wellness and forgiveness. This is a time for letting go of the past and embracing your future. Your past has been dim with lack of intelligence and awareness. Your future is bright with hope and awareness that you create it all.

As you move into your bright new future, you will begin to see the light and to know the light. It has been a long time since you have all, collectively, lived in the light. You will, however, prefer it to living in the darkness of fear. *Come to the Light of Love* is the title for our next book and I am certain you will love it. I bid you all a loving farewell until we meet in our next book.

God's Pen

I first heard the voice of God in 1988. I was sitting in my back yard reading a book when this big booming voice interrupted with, "I am God and I will not come to you by any other name." I felt like the voice was everywhere – inside of me as well as in the sky around me. I was so frightened that I ran in my bedroom to hide.

This was not the first time that I heard voices. I had been communicating with my own spirit guide or soul for about a year. I guess my depth of fear regarding God, and all that he represented to me at the time, was just too much.

I spent two days trying to avoid the voice of God, which was patiently waiting for me to respond. By the second day I was exhausted from lack of sleep and decided to give in and talk with him. This turned out to be the greatest gift and best decision of my life.

The first book, *God Spoke through Me to Tell You to Speak to Him*, shows my evolution from communicating with my soul to communicating with the Big Guy. It took a couple years for me to be comfortable communicating with God. My fear of a punishing God was big! That has most definitely changed and I now think of God as my partner and best friend.

In the beginning the voice of God would wake me in the middle of the night and tell me it was time to write. He said I had promised to do this work (I assumed he was talking about the soul/spirit me). I would drag myself up to a sitting position and watch in amazement as my hand flew across the page, while I tried to keep up by reading what was being written.

It was always so much fun to wake up the next morning and grab my notebook to see what God had written during the night. After some time the voice stopped waking me and I became comfortable picking up my pen and writing for God first thing in the morning. I think in the beginning I had to be awakened while still semi-conscious from sleep so I wouldn't object too much to the information that was being channeled through me.

As I grew less and less afraid (and more trusting) of God, he was able to communicate greater information. Some of the information is quit controversial, but I felt it important to just let it be and not censor it. I present the writings here to you as they were given to me. I have edited a little (mostly the more personal information regarding myself) and I have used a pen name for privacy reasons. I asked God for a good pen name and he guided me to Liane which (I was told) in Hebrew means "God has answered."

At one point I became a little concerned about my sanity in all this, so I went to a hypnotherapist to find out what I was doing. Under hypnosis I saw this incredibly huge beam of light with a voice coming from within it. It was a giant "loving light" and felt so comforting and kind. It felt like that's where I came from. After that I stopped worrying about my sanity. If this is crazy, I think it's a very good kind of crazy to be....

In loving light, Liane

Loving Light Books

Available at:
Loving Light Books: www.lovinglightbooks.com
Amazon: www.amazon.com
Barnes & Noble: www.barnesandnoble.com

Also Available on Request at Local Bookstores

www.ingramcontent.com/pod-product-compliance
Lightning Source LLC
LaVergne TN
LVHW011420080426
835512LV00005B/175